THE
STONEHENGE
SOLUTION

By the same author

THE CIRCLES EFFECT AND ITS MYSTERIES (*Artetech*)
CIRCLES FROM THE SKY (*Souvenir Press*)
THE GODDESS OF THE STONES (*Souvenir Press*)

THE STONEHENGE SOLUTION

Sacred Marriage and the Goddess

GEORGE TERENCE MEADEN

SOUVENIR PRESS

First published 1992 by Souvenir Press Ltd,
43 Great Russell Street, London WC1B 3PA
and simultaneously in Canada

ISBN 0 285 63057 1

Printed in Great Britain by
The Bath Press Ltd, Bath

Photoset by Rowland Phototypesetting Ltd
Bury St Edmunds, Suffolk

This book is dedicated to the genius who designed the sarsen stage of Stonehenge around 2000 BC, when Britain was green and pleasant and innocent, and who built it so well that today, three thousand years after its abandonment about 1000 BC, we are again able to admire the monument for its intended purpose. For Stonehenge was built to honour Love in a world of Peace, and to fulfil the eternal yearnings of humankind for security, fertility and immortality.

Contents

List of Illustrations

COLOUR PLATES

BLACK AND WHITE ILLUSTRATIONS

TABLES

Acknowledgements

First and foremost I thank my family for their endless encouragement during the long years of research which went into preparing this series of books on prehistory, beginning with *The Goddess of the Stones* and continuing now with *The Stonehenge Solution*. Since 1985, when I told my family of the secret of Stonehenge, I have worked relentlessly on the compelling drama that is the celebration of life known as the *hieros gamos*—that anciently sacred communion revealed as the Divine Marriage between the Great Goddess and her Sky God. During these exciting years I have visited hundreds of monuments and taken thousands of photographs, and two of the monuments, Stonehenge and Avebury—fortunately only thirty minutes' drive from my Wiltshire home—I have visited hundreds of times, both at dawn and by day. So I express my gratitude above all to my wife for her everlasting patience and for helping in the various archaeological, scientific and other causes which dominate my life as a result.

Dr Marija Gimbutas and Riane Eisler were equally enthusiastic, as were various other friends who in the last two years have been let into the Stonehenge secret as this book neared completion—in particular Brian Thomas, David Ashwell, and publisher Ernest Hecht. Finally I am happy to acknowledge the artistic skills of Maureen Oliver for painting the Stonehenge reconstructions and June Peel for six of the sketches. All the photographs are my own except for those credited with thanks to June Peel, H. R. Lambie, *The Salisbury Journal*, Colin and Janet Bord, and Anthony Weir.

Preface

The riddle of Stonehenge, the best-known prehistoric monument in the world, is solved.

Why was it built? How was it used? The principles which directed its planning are simple and sublime: no mathematics, no physics, no computer modelling, no stellar observations—just logic and the common sense of human experience.

The answers given in this book are arranged largely in the order in which I tackled the problems and worked them out, a process which ranged widely across the prehistoric world, at times far beyond Stonehenge.

I am a professional physicist and meteorologist, and an enthusiastic antiquarian specialising in the Neolithic and Bronze Ages throughout the world. In preparing for the Stonehenge challenge I thought that these qualifications would be useful but I knew that they were not enough in themselves. I also needed a good understanding of prehistoric symbolism and a global understanding of primitive religions. In order to perceive the monument as its builders did I had to enter into their state of mind, and this might well be complex because, as with all great feats of construction in prehistoric times, the driving force was religion. Cryptologists, detectives and others familiar with problem-solving and code-breaking will know that the best road to success begins by asking the right questions.

It has mistakenly and pessimistically been said that we can never know the religion of those forgotten peoples. The ancient Britons left us nothing in writing, no sagas, no known traditions; their period of activity was so long before the beginnings of recorded history that it might seem that nothing of potential use has come down to us. Nonetheless, the clues are there, and as one searches, so they multiply. Marshalled together and sensitively interpreted, they present an impressive picture of devout, hardworking communities faithful to their all-powerful divinity who was a fully fecund, resplendent female figure: the Great Goddess.

The first constructions at Stonehenge went up in the Neolithic farming period about 3200 BC, but the spiritual story began tens of thousands of years earlier in other parts of the world, in the formative stage of spiritual thought when men and women puzzled over the origins of life and what their fate would be after death. Understanding key factors of their religion leads us into the British New Stone Age, where we find the chief ideas symbolised and interpreted in the timeless stone of a megalithic building era—in the stone circles, the chambered barrows and the megalithic carvings. But before then, in the fourth millennium BC, another kind of field monument had appeared. Astonishing for their immense lengths, these were the ditch-and-bank constructions called cursuses which ran for mile after mile through England's virgin forests and ancient fields. Surprisingly, it was my solution to this little-known but substantial problem which led me successfully to Stonehenge. During the spring and summer of 1985, by dint of fieldwork, measurement and calculation, I solved the problem of the colossal Dorset Cursus with its network of Neolithic long barrows and bank barrows. After this, the enigmatic Stonehenge Cursus and its barrow complex was another exhilarating assignment whose basics were more swiftly evaluated.

Finally, one evening in October 1985 I returned afresh to the Stonehenge problem. Having by then established a general overview of the lost religion of the Great Goddess, and aided by my new understanding of the cursuses and other ancient British monuments, I applied the logic of the mounting evidence to the features and facts of Stonehenge. The solution came instantly. Everything fell into place, and the smaller puzzles were explained, too: why the Heel Stone was not on the Stonehenge axis, why the Heel Stone was placed outside the earthen circle, why the mineral of the Altar Stone was specially chosen, why three-stone arches predominated. Ever since, as the years have passed, I have carried out corroborative fieldwork, photography and the calculations indispensable to preparing my explanations for this series of books, and even now the work is not finished. At the same time I have worked on the unfolding crop-circle problem, itself a momentous discovery for physicists and prehistorians alike (see *The Circles Effect and its Mysteries*, 1989; *Circles from the Sky*, 1991), and the decipherment of the megalithic inscriptions and the origins and meanings of stone circles, round barrows and cups-and-rings in Britain and Ireland as described in *The Goddess of the Stones*, 1991.

And now Stonehenge gives up its secrets.

Superlative, brilliant, peerless Stonehenge—which I have cherished for so long in the beloved county of my birth since seeing the stones in 1945—will never be the same again. For six years in midsummer week I have explored Stonehenge after dawn, watching its magic at work. Everyone else who has journeyed there to ponder over its mysteries has stood in the wrong place, and looked the wrong way. Now that the truth is out, the intentions of its builders, all those thousands of years ago, will be revived. Stonehenge will start a new life and be admired again for what it used to be—an ageless monument to love and peace in the world of the Great Goddess.

G. Terence Meaden
Bradford-on-Avon,
Wiltshire.
1992.

Stonehenge in ruins, forever appealing with its age-old secrets. Why was is built?
How was it used?

1

The Wonder of Stonehenge

Even in its ruined state on the windswept plain in the heart of Wiltshire, Stonehenge, the finest achievement of the megalithic age, is a majestic sight which attracts two thirds of a million visitors every year. Its everlasting appeal stems partly from the very immensity of the stones, particularly the suspended lintels of the arches, but also from the circular symmetry of an anciently holy place, and from the eternal mystery that surrounds it. How and why was it built? What scenes has it witnessed?

Added to this is that singular charm which a monument gradually acquires when its perfection is marred, a feeling of ambivalent goodwill as for a proud and elderly statesman suffering the degeneracy of old age. If only the builders of Stonehenge could see it now, they would marvel, too, not at the poignancy of the beautiful ruin, but because of the perpetual puzzlement it brings. Last century Ralph Waldo Emerson wrote:

> He builded better than he knew
> The conscious stone to beauty grew.

His words were meant for Rome, but they apply better to Stonehenge.

If we still marvel at this abandoned ruin, how much greater must have been the wonder and fear that it inspired in the eyes of pious beholders and worshippers in those distant times; for they and their descendants revered the sanctuary for its profoundly spiritual values until its secrets vanished with the last of the peoples of the Late Bronze Age, around 1000 BC.

Then for three thousand years Stonehenge was silent, its worshippers gone, its purpose forgotten. The monument lay abandoned, crumbling before wind and weather, visited sporadically by the curious who could only stare and speculate as to why it was there.

'Upon no other subject, probably, have so many opinions been expressed, as upon Stonehenge,' declared the antiquarian Edward T. Stevens in 1882. Nothing has changed since. Opinions flow and ingenious hypotheses are advanced, but to no avail. This book, however, describes what I believe to be a breakthrough. The mists of time clear, and we can peer—as if through an opening window—into the depths of prehistory. At long last important questions are answered and we can begin to understand the monument's origins and purpose. That this has proved possible results from a new approach by which I tried to uncover the elements of the religion and the basis of the spirituality which lay behind the design and motivated the immense labours of its construction.

The efforts of my recent predecessors were directed at astronomical matters. Sometimes alignments were found between stone and stone, or stone and horizon, or stone and star, which may or may not have been intended by the planners; but despite the variety of conclusions reached the theme was monotonous. Any alignments were assumed to be a primary inspiration for placing the stones in position. The stones themselves had no meaning. Any motivations other than astronomy were thought secondary, unimportant, or else beyond our understanding. This approach has been fatal, and has led too many theorists into declaring that we are unlikely ever to know the true purpose of Stonehenge—or, for that matter, to decipher the majority of other outstanding monumental enigmas either.

I believe that it *is* possible to retreat in time, to think to some extent as our forebears did and, by uncovering some of the elements of the Neolithic religion, to re-create the basic ideas which inspired the planning of the monument. I have already described my findings in relation to circles, barrows, henges and megalithic art (see *The Goddess of the Stones*). In this book I shall concentrate on Stonehenge, Avebury, the cursuses and a few other monuments. What links them all is the discovery that in megalithic times neither a god nor a pantheon of gods was worshipped, but a goddess. She it was whose divine presence pervaded all nature—women, men, animals, earth and universe. At the beginning of the period which saw the birth of agriculture she was a fully fecund Great Goddess. There was then no Earth Mother in the agricultural sense; her rise, but only to a lesser power, came later, and on the way the Great Goddess

The distant Heel Stone seen through the middle archway on midsummer morning. The monument and its approach avenue are aligned on the point of sunrise for 2000 BC—not on the Heel Stone, a solitary megalith slightly off-axis and just outside the monument. If the Heel Stone did not mark the sunrise position, what purpose did it serve?

became a tri-function deity linked to the cycle of the seasons.

First of all, however, we have to go farther back in time, to see whether the Palaeolithic origins of the Goddess religion can be found in the sculptured objects and rock carvings from those far-off pre-agricultural days. The heritage of the Goddess was truly ancient, for her cult came to Britain following 20,000 years of continental Palaeolithic prehistory, eventually reaching the British Neolithic Age with its barrows and cursus earthworks, its chambered tombs, and its earthen, timber and megalithic circles.

Trying to understand these varied constructions has presented endless problems. None of the monuments are what they seem. Outwardly, all we can see are banks of earth stretching alongside straight or circular ditches. The circular types are called causewayed enclosures, henges, earthen circles, and round barrows, depending on their individual characteristics, place and age. The straight-sided monuments are mortuary enclosures, long barrows, and cursuses. Excavations produce pottery, artefacts, tools, and bones. Grave goods give clues about unknown religious customs. There are isolated standing stones and stone rows and avenues. There are rings of stone and rings of timber, stone cairns and stone houses, long houses and round houses. The monuments are numerous: nearly a thousand stone circles, forty thousand round barrows and cairns. The grave goods are studied, the clues multiply. But all the time most observers are not observing well enough.

Because so many sites contain bones, they have been called burial chambers or mortuary circles—mistakenly seen as abodes of the dead instead of temples for the living. Stone circles become dismal sites for ceremonial funerals instead of quiet or festive places for fertility cults, which they are more likely to be. Silbury is regarded as the tomb of a king instead of a seasonal centre cared for by a female divinity. Megalithic inscriptions are dismissed as having been carved without any underlying logic, so that the spirals, zigzags, cup-marks and lozenges of Ireland and Britain have too often been judged to be ornamentation for art's sake. Megalithic yards and precocious geometers have entered the arena. The ancient world has been overturned, obscured, by a surfeit of modern knowledge and an uncomprehending viewpoint. This blindness was foreseen by the great Romanian historian of religions, Mircea Eliade, who said that to understand the lost religions we must enter the mind of the primitive. Admittedly, the dead and the living do sometimes come together in circles, on round hills, in chambered barrows, but they do so more for the sake and the future prosperity of the living —not solely for solemn burials and macabre ceremonials. Immortality aspirations and fertility needs were the compelling forces which moved the stones, not death and burial rites.

What building traditions existed at the time of the founding of the henge of Stonehenge when the circular bank was raised? In Britain around 3200 BC there were the causewayed enclosures, the chambered and earthen long barrows, the linear cursuses. There were wooden circles, but few if any stone circles. Ireland had 'passage-grave' temples, including magnificent Dowth, Knowth and Newgrange in the Boyne Valley, County Meath. Ireland's megalithic building era peaked before 3000 BC; Britain's would peak several hundred years later.

What did these peoples know that we do not, which impelled them to undertake public works on a scale so colossal that it was at the extreme limits of their primitive technology? The cause of our ignorance is the same as that which prevented other modern thinkers from grasping the solution to these ancient wonders: fifteen hundred years ago Christianity reached these islands, displacing religions which were themselves the degenerate successors to the megalithic

Goddess religion—that much older faith which rose to glory in the period between 4000 and 1000 BC.

In megalithic times the female deity was all-powerful. *She* was the object of worship which drove men to move stones and mountains, to raise temples and shrines in her honour. She was the Great Goddess. As a product of Nature she symbolised Nature in all her aspects. Hers was the cycle of life by which all living forms were born from the earth and went back to it at death to be born again. By the time the Christian missionaries arrived, she had long been supplanted as the primary deity. The Celts had substituted a pantheon dominated by male gods, but she survived in a form of Earth Mother under names such as Anu, Brigit, Brigid and Bride. The missionaries and converts could not immediately annihilate such a well-loved figure. Her places of worship and festive celebrations were Christianised: churches were raised in some henges and alongside standing stones; Christian symbols were carved on Goddess Stones; Eostre's spring festival became the Christian Easter, and the New Year festival of the winter solstice was chosen to mark Christ's Nativity. The Earth Mother lived on in popular belief, especially in deep rural areas, and fertility rituals continued to be practised by agricultural communities because Christianity could not give children to barren women or ensure easy labour as the old ways had seemingly done. From time to time there were persecutions, when a perverted Christian doctrine did all it could to suppress the lingering folklore and the popular superstitions. The stones of Avebury suffered two shameful attacks—in the fourteenth and eighteenth centuries. Unlucky women throughout Western Europe were declared witches to gratify the demands of a male society worshipping a 'jealous' male god—and in the course of three centuries some eight million innocent victims were tortured and murdered.

The total dominance of Christianity closed men's minds. Men made the religious laws and the secular laws. Women had no rights to property, no means of voicing themselves. One half of humanity was enslaved and only now, centuries later, is it breaking free. History books were written by men; the truth was distorted. The professions were filled by men who knew nothing of the pre-Christian mind. God-fearing antiquarians and archaeologists led the way in calling the prehistoric tribes of Britain and Ireland barbarians. Until recently prehistorians had no feeling for the spiritual sensitivities of those distant peoples, no wish to entertain the idea that Britain formerly lived in peace under the protection of a mother figure. Only now, in these newly liberal times, can we begin to accept the evidence of the monuments for what it really tells us: that a Goddess was worshipped for thousands of years, that fertility practices were a normal part of life throughout pre-Christian times, and that there was *never* anything in any sense obscene about them—as Hindus today would candidly affirm—for sexuality was regarded as the divine motivating power of the universe and its suppression was an autocratic decision of the male Church leaders.

At last, without fear or shame, we can discuss the likely truths of the long-lost religion which involved tender and honest beliefs in the everlasting cycles of birth, life, death and rebirth. The early story of the Great Goddess will lead us to grasp the true significance of those ancient monuments which for so long amazed us.

2

The Universal Womb

Around ten thousand years ago, in the Neolithic era of Eastern Europe, the practice of cultivation began. The control and exploitation of cereal crops gave a measure of security to tribes who until then had relied for food on chance discoveries of seeds and fruits and occasional success in the hunt.

The seeds planted in the receptive earth passed through a cycle of growth, ripening and decay; for the first time humans played a part in regulating nature's life forces. The idea was born that the help of the deities had to be invoked because the agricultural cycle was part of the cosmic cycle which itself was integrated with the divine. Above all, the aid of the Great Goddess was sought, especially that part of her domain which was to become the province of the Earth Mother. With her help the risk of crop failure was minimised, the harvest made bountiful, the animals rendered fruitful. Without it, the seasons were irregular, the weather inclement, the routine endangered. And so it was that, in all agrarian societies throughout the world, practical knowledge of developing farming techniques came to be supplemented by sacred rituals.

The Goddess was universal. Soil and earth were her body. Just as life issues forth at birth so is life reclaimed at death, for Earth is both womb and grave, at once fertile and protective. The reverence shown to the Earth by struggling farmers was due to Earth's inexhaustible productiveness; and the mystical link between soil fertility and woman's generative functions was the inescapable consequence.

Entering the grave, or going into a cave, was like returning to the womb. In Sumerian *matu* meant 'womb', 'underworld', and 'sacred cave' from the universal root for 'mother'—hence Latin and pre-Teutonic *mater*, and Old Teutonic *modar*. The relation between hole and ground or orifice and cliff was that of vulva and womb.

The cave was shelter and the cave was home—a haven from tempest, a place eminently suited to human birth. The same applied to the wigwam, the log hut, the stone house: they were artificial caves raised on the surface of the earth, the Goddess's body. Going home meant returning to the security of the Goddess's womb, a reassurance which made both life and death meaningful. The doorway was the vulva, chosen by enlightened peoples to face the midwinter sunrise, so that it might admit and secure the rays of the New Year sun. The fixing of the solar alignments of various structures (tombs, temples, homes, and other buildings) was a widespread practice, but there is little use in remarking on this unless we also try to understand the reason why such things were done. To succeed we must enter into the mental universe of those deeply religious societies and discover the nature of their beliefs and ideals. Then, what appeared eccentric becomes regular, what was ugly becomes beautiful, what was inexplicable becomes coherent, and what some call obscene becomes proper.

Whereas the Neolithic Age saw the ascendancy of the Earth Goddess within the Great Goddess's universe, fertility goddesses had been worshipped long before then. For thousands of years, in the Mesolithic and the Upper Palaeolithic eras, creator-fertility images dominated prehistoric sculptural art and rock engravings. Best known are the female statuettes of central Europe, which display the female form with exaggerated emphasis on the womanly features—the pregnant belly, the large buttocks, the heavy thighs. Vulvas and pubic triangles are often indicated, whereas breasts are less often amplified than 'modern' thinking might expect. This would imply that, apart from the primary desire for fertility, the sculptor's intention related to fears regarding the precariousness of the life-giving side of human birth. Such a statuette represented the fertile Great Goddess as she was to be viewed: the content of the Feminine at the time of easy pregnancy and safe delivery. It amounted to an appeal as to how she should function.

The so-called Venus de Laussel, a figure 43 cm (17 inches) high, was carved on the outer wall at the entrance of a cave or rock shelter in the Dordogne. Its date would be between 25000 and 20000 BC. There is a horn in the figure's right hand, with thirteen notches cut into it, which may correspond to the thirteen months of the lunar calendar. In these remote times the horn may have served as a symbol related to the horned moon, and certainly it is true that the moon was more highly revered than any other object of nature. The Moon Goddess

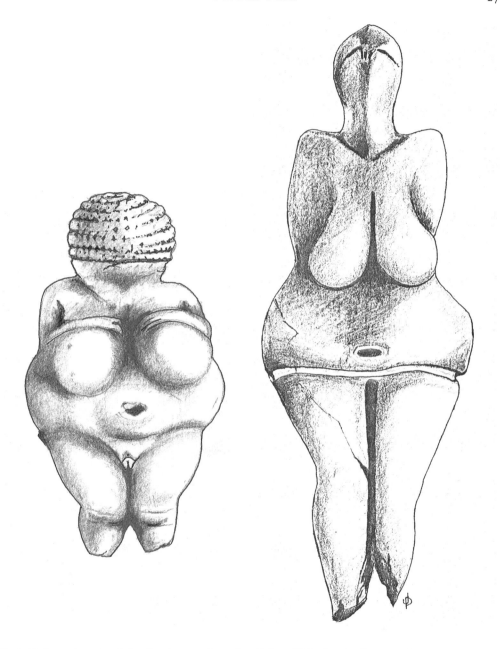

Two of many female statuettes known from the Palaeolithic Age in Central Europe. *Left*: a Goddess carved in limestone from Willendorf, Austria, roughly dated to 25000–30000 BC. *Right*: a Goddess made of baked clay, from Dolni Vestonice, Moravia.

was another side to the Great Goddess; in full view of the watching world she underwent a pregnant waxing and waning on a monthly cycle similar to the feminine menstrual cycle. Moon and woman were mystically united. The celestial divinity was Life-giver, caring for the female provider of childlife.

Such sculptures reveal a highly developed artistic sense, an achievement which could hardly have appeared 'overnight'. They would have been preceded by less well executed carvings, perhaps over vast periods of time. J. Munsch has recorded triangular pieces of flint from the Early Palaeolithic which had breasts and vulvas crudely sculpted on them by simple knapping (a photograph has been reproduced by Marija Gimbutas in *The Language of the Goddess*). Dating them by tool association suggests that they could be half a million years old. Not only is this vitally important as evidence of early artistic ability, but it proves how old ideas centred on Goddess worship might be.

Reverence for female fertility from those early times was also formalised by the carving of vulvas into the rocks of Aurignacian cave shelters. As Marija Gimbutas emphasises, the vulvas stood for the divinity, the essential part standing for the whole. The vulvar images of stone 'symbolise the vulva and womb of the goddess'. Archaeologists date the oldest of these engravings, by association, to 30000 BC or a little later. Examples can be seen in the caves of Abri Blanchard and La Ferrassie in the Vezère Valley not far from Les Eyzies in southern France. The vulvas, occasionally reddened with ochre, signified the

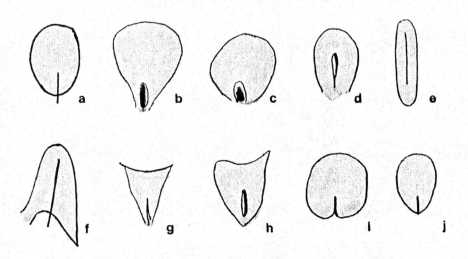

Vulvas engraved on rock surfaces in Upper Palaeolithic caves. (a), (b) and (c) Abri Blanchard; (d), (e) and (h) La Ferrassie; (f) El Castillo; (g) Pergouset; (i) Laussel; (j) Lalinde.

association of the caves with the womb of the Goddess. In a cave in the Spanish Pyrenees, at El Castillo, red-painted vulvas can be seen which date from the Early Magdalenian (around 15–17000 BC). In the same panel, painted black, is a flower or branched tree. Plant and vulvas share the symbolism of birth and

This painting on a cave wall at El Castillo, Santander, Northern Spain, shows five vulvas, each half-a-metre high, painted red. The plant-like feature is black.

growth. Besides colouring engraved vulvas in this fashion, entire niches and fissures in caves used in prehistoric times have been found painted in red ochre. This suggests that natural clefts and niches were seen as likenesses of the human vulva, which of course stressed their intended use as Goddess vulvas.

Not surprisingly, any natural cleft in a cliff or split in a rock provided similar motivation for Goddess worship. Crevices attracted attention in all archaic societies, and have continued to do so right into our own century. A naturally-formed cleft in a rocky outcrop at Crawford Ranch, Canebrake Wash in San Diego county, was venerated by South California Indians as the Earth Mother's vulva. On the summit of the Wrekin in Shropshire is a cleft called the Needle's Eye. Folklore has it that girls squeezing through should not look back if they want to

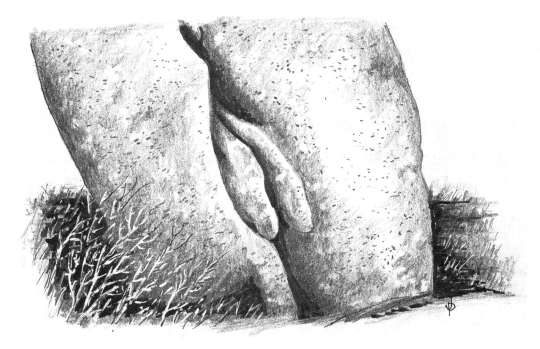

A natural cleft in a rock at Canebrake Wash in San Diego county, Southern California, an obvious site for Goddess worship.

get married, and that their boyfriends should greet them with a kiss on the other side. These simple ideas hint at a deeper meaning born in an ancient fertility rite. Again the journal *Folklore* records that in the Highland region of Scotland, near Dingwall, there are two boulders in the Brahan Wood which lean against each other, meeting at the top. An old woman who died quite recently remembered that when she was a child she had a fit which her parents thought to be epileptic. So they took her to the leaning stones and lit a fire at the top, then passed her through the opening below.

It is the same with fissures in the ground. They attracted attention as symbols of the Goddess, eminently suitable as oracular openings and places of worship. In Greece the Delphi oracle was so named because not only did the word 'delphi' mean womb, but the site had a feature whose shape related to this. The same applied to standing stones which were naturally-fissured or artificially-grooved. In North Yorkshire there are three stones, known as the Devil's Arrows, standing nearly in line. They have deep grooves running down from their tops, which appear to be artificial, but are more likely the result of the weathering of softer strata in the rock. If the latter, the stones were deliberately selected because of

The fissured stones at Boroughbridge in North Yorkshire. In Christian times they came to be known as the Devil's Arrows, but when originally erected they must have been venerated as signs of the Goddess. *Photo Janet and Colin Bord*

this property. One of the Nine Stones, a prehistoric circle on Harthill Moor in Derbyshire, is similarly scored. A fissured menhir in Wales, Maen y Cleddau, was also possibly selected for its shape. These grooved stones may all have been Goddess Stones. The intensity of the imagery can explain why Goddess-worshipping societies from Stonehenge to Orkney chose to decorate their pottery with multiple grooved lines, to such a degree that archaeologists call the pottery

Grooved Ware and its makers the Grooved Ware people. It is likely that in addition to the spiral and the lozenge, which came to symbolise the Goddess widely in the Neolithic Age, the groove also performed this function, whether incised on megaliths, plaques, or pots.

Perforated stones, artificial or not, attracted similar attention from the Neolithic farmer. The Bole Stone, Crouse (South-West Scotland), the Tolven Stone (Cornwall) and Men-an-Tol (also Cornwall) are among surviving holed stones in Britain, Ireland and France. Hundreds have been destroyed over the centuries, many in uncomprehending purges. One, known as the Ring Stone, at the Avebury circles in Wiltshire, was eliminated only a few years before William Stukeley's first visit in 1719. The usual custom with holed stones was to crawl through the hole if it was big enough, or to pass children through, with the expectation of curing illnesses. Newborn infants were blessed in the same way. The symbolism is the *yoni*, the Goddess's vulva providing strength through the sympathetic shape of its immutable stone. Cures were expected because the rite related to rebirth. By the same token the Goddess Ring ended sterility. In Grampian a pierced stone, the Devil's Needle, remains in use today, where barren women used to crawl through the hole as a fertility rite, and still do so for luck.

Caves spell out the vulva symbolism just as clearly. Their use through Palaeolithic times and into the Neolithic era meant more than just physical shelter from the elements; they provided sacred shelter from the dangerous outer world, for every cave was a sanctuary to the Goddess. There were thousands in France of which some, as already noted, were marked with vulvar signs. In South Wales, Goat's Cave at Paviland had an elaborate ritual grave beneath its floor. The person buried there, about 20000 BC, with shell necklace, mammoth skull and ivory—the bones painted with red ochre to symbolise life—had been returned to the womb of the Goddess.

The crevice or cleft remains today a popular, well-recognised symbol for the vulva. Besides its universal recognition in the conch and the cowrie, and its everyday appearance in the indispensable grain of wheat, there is the popular gesture of the finger sign with thumb between index and middle fingers. Very likely this ancient sign, known to the Romans more for coarseness and jollity rather than offensiveness, was not reckoned too salacious until our patriarchal, male-god-worshipping society decided that it should be suppressed because of its undercurrent Goddess symbolism. Since the complete message denotes conjugal union, in a prehistoric Goddess society such a sign would more likely have conveyed genuine goodwill, a salute for health and fertility at a time when these were the foremost desires of an innocent, peaceful rural population.

Similar, if not worse, treatment has been meted out to the word 'cunt', a perfectly normal, useful word with a linguistic heritage and literary functions, which was in proper use until a puritanical government legislated against it and other 'Anglo-Saxon' words. This followed a series of vicious witch hunts encouraged by an evil establishment wishing to suppress what amounted to apparent signs of surviving Goddess beliefs. According to Michael Dames, J. S. Farmer in his *Dictionary of Slang* confirms that the word is 'a true language word of the oldest stock', in company with Latin *cunnus*, Middle English *cunte*, Old Norse *kunta*, Old Frisian *kunte*, and, above all, Basque *kuna* where ethnology implies a kinship of the present-day Basque countryman with the far-off Neo-lithic peoples. Between Avebury and Hungerford the River Kennet was called the Cunnt (or Cunnit) by the locals until 1740 at least. Michael Dames logically proposes that the name of the stream derived from the obvious orifice which is the source of the Swallowhead spring between Silbury Hill and West Kennet long barrow. In view of the proven involvement of the Goddess with Silbury his observation is astute, and adds support to my belief in a society worshipping the fertile Goddess in that part of Wiltshire in Neolithic times. In line with Michael Dames, Barbara Walker says that 'English words like cunning, kenning, and ken (knowledge) descended from a spectrum of words related to cunt, which in turn was the Great Goddess Cunti'. The same goes for words like country, cunicle, and incunabula.

It is common, of course, for water to issue from natural holes, notably the pure water of springs or of underground streams. These were venerated throughout prehistory and well into recorded history, stemming from mankind's eternal need for water. Recognised as the source of life, the spring and well were held sacred to the Goddess who commanded their powers. Their reverence has continued into modern times, even surviving the prohibitions of Christian doctrines aimed at suppressing them. A tenth-century canon directed: 'We enjoin every priest . . . totally extinguish every heathenism; and forbid . . . well-worshippings, and the vain practices which are carried on with various spells'. Thus wells and springs, which are rather innocently regarded by most people in today's world, owe their continued attention to Goddess beliefs in pre-Christian times, when the female principle was honoured within what had begun in the Neolithic as a more balanced, warless society. The mediaeval priests who followed the direction of Rome condemned well-worship and other rustic, non-Christian customs associated with Goddess vulva beliefs, using the Latin words *cunnus diaboli*, the cunt of the devil. The Church had invented the concept of a devil, drawing the name from Sanskrit *devi* (which remains in use in the Indo-Orient as an honourable and beautiful word), Greek *diabolos* and Latin *diva*, all meaning goddess, to explain the continuance of a world of sin and violence. For two thousand years the Judaeo-Christian tradition has abhorred sexuality and love which were the province of the peace-loving Goddess, and it is our inheritance that violence is tolerated or encouraged (both in drama and war) while natural sexuality is mocked and suppressed.

The well-dressing ceremonies which persist in Britain to this day, notably at numerous village wells in Derbyshire and Staffordshire, had their beginnings in the Age of the Goddess. It is through Goddess-inspired superstitions, maintained by the tradition of folklore, that coins continue to be tossed into wells, fountains or running water as good-luck tokens or offerings. Unknowingly, these habits are but a sweet relic of a bygone age when 'God was a woman'. The Christian genius was to reconsecrate the popular wells and springs in the name of (usually) a female saint, and in due course to deify Mary in order to fill the gap left by the vanishing Goddess. Thus we find in Pembrokeshire, within a 'Goddess cleft' between limestone cliffs, the well of St Govan. Even in Celtic times, two thousand years after the Neolithic-Bronze Age transition, when the Romans reached Britain, one local divinity governing the waters was the sun Goddess Sul or Sulis. The era of the dominion of the unique Great Goddess had long ended and a degenerate pantheon had taken over. These were so-called 'heroic' times when men dominated the world and male gods were in the ascendancy. A curse inscribed in Latin on a lead tablet was found in the Goddess's hot spring at Bath, the South of England town known to the Romans as *Aquae Sulis* (The Waters of Sul): 'Docilianus . . . to the most holy Goddess Sulis. I curse him who has stolen my hooded cloak, whether man or woman, slave or free, that the Goddess Sulis [will] not allow [him] sleep or children . . . until he has returned the cloak to the temple of her divinity'. The holy well at Glastonbury, Somerset, had its origins in pre-Christian times when, because the water is tinted red by iron-oxide impurities, it was viewed as the Goddess's menstrual-affected waters. The Church sought to terminate the Goddess connection at this place by annexing the sacred well and shrine and Christianising the legend.

For tens of thousands of years, throughout which the highest respect was paid to the Life-giving Goddess, the vulva-cave was a retreat offering safety, a place for repose. This enormous time-span of committed reverence for a female divinity was devoid of any obvious signs of the genuine worship of a male deity. Male imagery does occasionally appear, but chiefly in a subordinate or allied role denoting fertilising powers, rather than as an icon of some male god. Cave drawings have been found in Spain and France and clay phalluses in French Upper Palaeolithic caves at Laussel in the Dordogne and Tuc d'Audoubert, Ariège.

Caves with stalactites and stalagmites inspired a very special devotion from Palaeolithic and Neolithic races. Here the Goddess's life-waters could be seen in the process of *creating* life pillars of rock from the rock—phallic-like forms

The pillar crypt beneath St Wystan's Church, Repton, Derbyshire—Goddess/
womb symbolism appropriated by Christianity and re-created in Saxon architecture.
Photo Janet and Colin Bord

which became natural pillar shrines to the concentrated, regenerative life processes. Marija Gimbutas explains that subterranean crypts with a central pillar surrounded by offerings were commonplace in the Goddess-worshipping Minoan communities of the third and second millennia. In the palace of Knossos, Crete, stone columns were marked with Goddess symbols of regeneration and rebirth, indicating that 'pillar crypts symbolised the womb of the Goddess Creatrix, where transformation from death to life took place and where initiation rites were performed. The participants returned to the womb—that is "died"—and after the ceremonies were reborn again.' The pillar crypts of the early Christian Church unwittingly or deliberately took over this Goddess/womb symbolism—and then suppressed it, an idea that had begun more than twenty thousand years earlier with simple stalactite/stalagmite caves which were moist and humid like the human womb.

3

Womb, Tomb and Temple

Burial after death is the returning of the deceased to the care of the Goddess. In early times it was usual to curve the corpse in imitation of the foetal position. The desire was rebirth: like the planted seed which grows anew, a fresh beginning could be expected. In the Neolithic Age most burials were in long mounds or chambered tombs of earth and stone. Raising the mound created a womb, and sealing it interred the corpse within the Goddess's body. And as the chamber was the womb, so the entrance passage and door were vagina and vulva. T. Cyriax, in 1921, was perhaps the first archaeologist to remark on this:

> The earth under which men [and women] are buried is the mother of the dead. The object of the tomb builder would have been to make the tomb as much like the body of a Mother as he was able. The same idea seems to have been carried out in the internal arrangements of the passage grave, with the burial chambers and passage perhaps representing uterus and vagina.

Indeed, many of the chambered barrows were more than just womb-tombs; they were womb-temples, sacred places for rites and worship ruled by the Goddess.

In France a tradition of megalithic long-barrow building developed from the fifth millennium BC onwards, significantly earlier than in the British Isles. Goddess images with recognisable human features appeared on some of the big

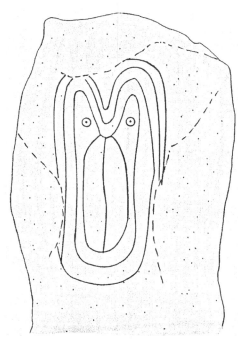

The Great Goddess represented by a vulva. This Goddess Stone is in a dolmen *coudée* at Luffang, near Crac'h, in Brittany.

stones and this makes it easy for us to see them as Goddess Stones. Some of the other carvings whose abstract qualities made them less easy for non-specialists to recognise were clearly vulvas. The figure from Luffang, Crac'h, in the west of Brittany near Carnac, is one example. The solitary vulva epitomises the whole goddess.

At Gavrinis, an island off the west coast of Brittany, not far from Locmaria-quer and Carnac, the walls of the great fourth-millennium temple-tomb seem to be covered in vulvas and, as a consequence, fertility symbolism. When this megalithic masterpiece was built it lay on a peninsula. Then, as now, it must have been an exciting place of pilgrimage for Goddess worshippers. Facing south-east, its façade is slightly crescent-shaped, and its aspect allows the mid-winter rising sun to penetrate the dark interior of the monument through a low, vulvar entrance. Stooping, one follows the entrance passage for six metres, past heavily-carved orthostats lining the sides. The stones are of dark granite, a colour which evokes the darkness of the moist womb, for black was the colour of fertility in pre-Christian times (just as white was the colour of bone, and therefore of

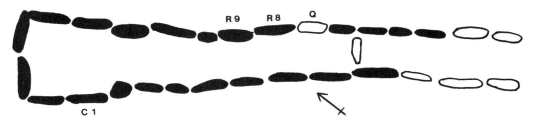

The Goddess temple on the island called Gavrinis, off the west coast of Brittany, contains the finest carved murals of Neolithic France. The long gallery and end-chamber are the womb-passage and womb of the Great Goddess. The decorated slabs are shown black. Only the quartz stone Q and the stones near the entrance are undecorated. Stones C1, R8 and R9 are illustrated in this book.

death). But the hard stone, an exacting medium in which to work using nothing more than simple hardstone tools, was elaborately carved. The curving lines which flow in multiple arcs and bands create an impression of movement and vitality as they sweep across nearly every stone of the gallery-passage and the inner womb-chamber. Yet the rising, repetitive, flowing arcs are not round circles, nor are they parts of spirals (although four complete spirals can be found among them all). As parts of elongated glistening circles, their effect is both surprising and mystifying. Why are they there? What did they mean? Whatever else, impressionable, free-thinking, intelligent observers have probably always had an intuition that somehow they touch upon the traditional mysteries of woman—as I did at the time of my visit in 1987 with Aubrey Burl, Stephen Morris, and a group of others.

Now, as the secrets of the lost Goddess religion are progressively unravelled, I find them easier to understand. Gavrinis *is* a temple to the Great Goddess, probably the most meaningful known site in France. Its images, architecturally and artistically, are those of woman triumphant in her life-giving powers. The panels are artistic vulvar representations exalting the generative forces; labia, vagina, clitoris, are compellingly portrayed in the black, gleaming medium. The repetition of the motifs, panel after panel, reinforces the message. The Neolithic visitor, on following the passage and reaching the womb, must have been stunned by the power of the symbolism—as we are today once we understand it. For too long this place has been called a tomb although no bones were found in it. No, it never was a sepulchre; it was a place of worship, a temple, a shrine. Standing at the head of a peninsula, it faced the Atlantic Ocean which in some mythologies could have been looked upon as the waters of the amniotic ocean. Marija Gimbutas was among the first to recognise the uterine nature of this great monument

Above: Vulvar symbolism artistically portrayed on stone R9 at Gavrinis. There is a primary central vulva with supplementary vulvas and multifold arcs to highlight their importance by magnifying the effect.

Right: On stone R8 the vulvas rise and multiply, reinforcing the fundamental message.

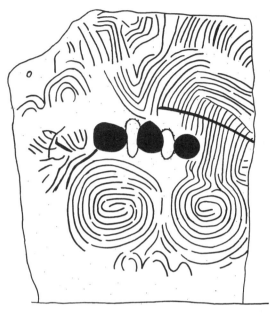

Stone C1 at Gavrinis. Spiral forms expand and rise on a stone dominated by the presence of three deep pits or cup-marks scored into its surface.

and to call it a tomb-womb and sanctuary, and I am calling it a womb-temple.

The first stone on the left on entering the chamber, C1, is important for its triple circular depressions reminiscent of cup-marks. In *The Goddess of the Stones* I explained how the triple cup-marks on the midsummer sunset stone at Newgrange represent the triple-function Goddess. Below the triple cup-feature at Gavrinis are two spiral carvings, right-handed in sense. Another stone, the seventh from the entrance along the right-hand side of the gallery, is of splendid white quartz. Although it is one of the few undecorated stones at Gavrinis it is a major Goddess Stone. Aubrey Burl has pointed out that the passage and entrance are angled so that this stone could be illuminated at the extreme southern rising of the moon, which happens every 18 years, as well as at the annual midwinter sunrise. The annual arrival of the midwinter sun is an important element, as it is at Newgrange. But why, and what did it mean?

Not far away, at Locmariaquer, is a megalithic monument known as La Table des Marchands, inside which is a mural engraving which Marija Gimbutas correctly assigns to Goddess-vulva worship. Covering the huge triangular stone are rows of hooks or crooks, interpreted by symbologists as images of energy and regeneration, ranged on either side of a central vulvar-framed cup-mark sign. This cup-mark shows up well in oblique lighting and is easy to spot once pointed

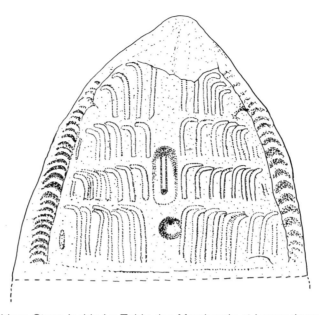

The great Goddess Stone inside La Table des Marchands at Locmariaquer in western Brittany.
This enormous block is the terminal mural of an important Goddess shrine or temple.
Centred about the half-metre long vulva is an array of Goddess hooks—every one an emblem
of energy and regeneration.

out. The repeated use of the crook-symbol in the design, together with the triangle, by suggesting the idea of pubic hair intensifies the message: that the tableau is a Goddess icon prepared for solemn veneration at a place of Goddess worship.

Obvious vulvas appear too in the fourth-millennium megalithic art of Ireland. There is one on orthostat 49 in the western passage of the twin-passage temple-tomb of Knowth, and another in the vulvar design on a 50-cm long portable object, an engraved piece of sandstone which George Eogan diffidently described as a 'baetyl'—a sacred phallic stone.

The spiral is another Goddess image, particularly when left-handed, and carries its own vulvar symbolism (see *The Goddess of the Stones*). The vulva also appears in other abstract forms, notably as a lozenge or 'diamond' in the religious art of the Irish Neolithic period, and in Anglesey, Scotland, and England. Its use as a Goddess symbol was widespread and continued into the Bronze Age period of Stonehenge.

In Britain a tradition of long barrow building evolved later than in Brittany. British long barrows date from the fourth millennium and continued in use well into the third millennium. The word 'barrow', from the Old English *beorg*,

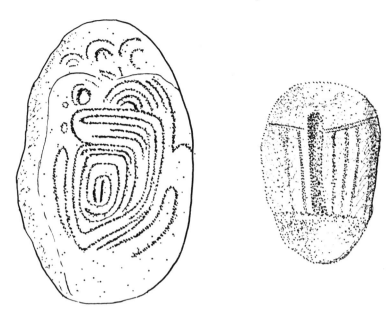

Two Goddess Stones with central vulvas from Knowth in County Meath, Ireland. *Left*: from a stone in the western passage; *right*: a portable sandstone block, half a metre long.

means low hill. Long barrows are frequently orientated in a generally eastward direction, mostly between south-east and north-east. This indicates some mystical regard for the direction of the rising sun, especially in connection with chambered long barrows. Of the non-solar-orientated exceptions, the majority are earthen barrows on the chalk downs of Dorset and the Stonehenge area of Wiltshire. By contrast, these exceptions form unique patterns of their own and are a vital ingredient of this book.

In the stonier areas of the British Isles and Brittany, long barrows and passage-graves often had central passages and one or more chambers. Because bones have been found in them they have usually been thought of as houses of the dead, but these barrows, too, resemble the womb of the Goddess, so they must surely have been built as temples to benefit the living. Excavation has shown that when the barrows came to be sealed in antiquity after centuries of use, some of them contained large numbers of skulls and bones but rarely complete skeletons, especially articulated skeletons. Corpse decomposition *in situ* leads to an articulated, ordered arrangement of bones. The finding of non-articulated bones indicates disturbance and rearrangement. Indeed many are usually missing, the long bones and skulls being most often found. This tells us something of the purpose behind barrow construction. The barrow takes on the air of a repository, a place where older bones get pushed aside to make room for later arrivals. Moreover, the later entries are not so much a complete corpse as a selection of bones which had been dried elsewhere, perhaps in a charnel house, before being brought into the barrow.

How can such a place be called a tomb when by its shape it seems to have been built as an extension of the womb of the Goddess? The construction plan of passage-graves and chambered barrows so often mimics female reproductive organs. Michael Dames offered examples from Neolithic Malta, and Marija Gimbutas found other examples from Neolithic Europe, ranging from Yugoslavia, Sicily and Sardinia to France, Ireland and Poland. Several shrines like this date from around 6000 BC. In 1924 Edward J. Burrow drew attention to the similarity of construction plans between the English long barrows at Uley and Stoney Littleton and the Maltese temple at Tarxien. 'Such a resemblance can hardly be accidental, and shows there to have been a definite architectural design for these prehistoric burial-mounds, probably associated with certain religious rites and formulae.' Edward Burrow saw the importance of similarity of shape; Michael Dames and T. Cyriax understood why.

In Britain, Ireland and Brittany many long barrows are clearly aligned on the midwinter rising sun, others less obviously so. One such example is the Cotswold-Severn barrow at Stoney Littleton near Bath. The precise alignment of the gallery on midwinter sunrise originally went unnoticed, doubtless because the steepness of the hill causes a much delayed sunrise. This was no mere tomb to its builders; it was another womb-shaped temple.

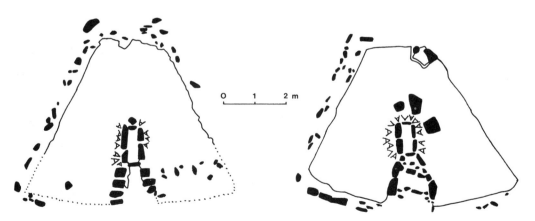

Plans of two shrines at Lepenski Vir, Yugoslavia. Marija Gimbutas pointed out that these are Goddess representations, the forecourt areas corresponding to the space between the Goddess's legs and the inner space to her womb.

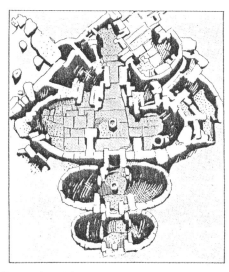
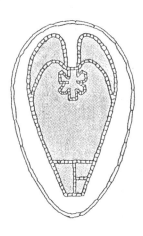

General architectural similarities between the Tarxien temples in Malta and Cotswold-Severn chambered long barrows such as Hetty Pegler's Tump at Uley. Each has a medial vagina gallery and a uterine interior divided into smaller chambers.

The remains of the Goddess Temple, or court tomb, at Creevykeel, County Sligo, looking from the vagina-womb gallery through the vulva, formed by the trilithon arch, into the court —the nearly-enclosed area between the Goddess's legs. *Photo Anthony Weir, Janet and Colin Bord.*

Stoney Littleton lies between the Mendips and the Cotswolds, part of the fossil-bearing Jurassic belt that crosses England from Devon to eastern England. All the stones of the gallery and chambers of the barrow are oolitic slabs, obtained by splitting from a local outcrop or quarry. The barrow's stones abound with fossils, most notably *Gryphaea* (a kind of curled-up oyster known in folklore as the Devil's toe-nail), brachiopods, and ammonites well-known for their spiral-centred shells.

To judge by the strategic positions occupied by the stone slabs which bear the barrow's largest ammonite impressions, it seems obvious that these slabs were chosen and their positions decided by their petrified spirals. One of them, 20 centimetres in diameter, stands in the passage at the entrance to the first cell on the right. The other, technically the negative-cast of the creature, decorates the south-west door-jamb. The original diameter of this ammonite must have been close to 32 centimetres (13 inches).

In common with other chambered barrows of the Cotswold-Severn type, the stone-lined forecourt is curved into the shape of a pair of horns, gently evoking not only the imagery of bull-horns but the holy horns of the crescent moon. Moreover, the vagina-gallery is aligned to correspond exactly with the point of the rising sun on midwinter's day. Every year for just a few minutes the sun shines to the end of the long passage and a few moments later illuminates, on

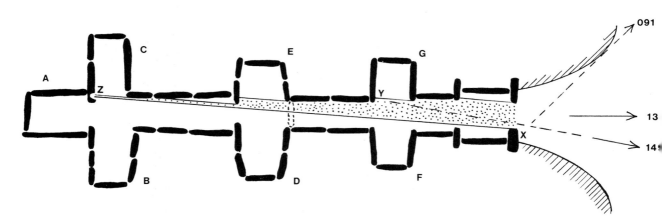

Plan of Stoney Littleton long barrow. The seven chambers are labelled A–G, following Arthur Bulleid. The vagina-gallery faces the midwinter sunrise (138 degrees from north) and allows a shaft of sunlight to illuminate the Goddess cup Z at the entrance to chamber C. X and Y mark the positions of prominent ammonite fossils. Fossil Y, which catches the midwinter sunshine annually, is so placed that it can only be illuminated by the moon at its extreme southerly rising (149 degrees from north).

the right-hand side, part of a specially-selected stone which bears a deep, broad, natural cup-mark. It is not obvious from simple compass measurements that this is so. For a level horizon the sun rises close to 128 degrees from north, but because the barrow faces up a steep incline the sunrise is delayed until 138 degrees is reached. At that moment the sun bursts over the hilltop and shines brightly down the middle of the Goddess barrow, soon after which the cup-mark is reached. Why was it so important to get the sun's energy into the depth of the womb in this way, and at this season?

A second alignment concerns the ammonite spiral at the entrance to cell G. The full moon illuminates this fossil in midsummer at intervals of 18 years, when it rises at its most southerly azimuth of the Metonic cycle.

Several symbolic aspects of the contemporary religion were designed into the architectural features of this unified Goddess-womb construction. There were the fossilised spirals of death and of rebirth, the mystic cup-mark (whose spiritual meaning is explored in *The Goddess of the Stones*), the curving forecourt, the alignment on the midwinter solstice, the extreme lunar alignment, and the fossil remains of petrified life-forms. The superabundance of life-death symbolism and Goddess womb symbolism indicates that the barrow was more than a place for the dead. It was a shrine for the living, and its major cosmic alignments prove an intimate relationship between Sky and Earth as if it was built as the house

Looking from the depths of the womb of the Goddess at Stoney Littleton, showing the small area of sky into which the sun rises at its winter solstice.

The long forecourt entrance of Hetty Pegler's Tump at Uley leads to the Goddess's womb-opening, positioned to receive the sun at midwinter sunrise.

and womb of the Goddess to await the annual return of the sun. One senses here the presence of a rite which calls for the annual renewal of the world and its life-forms.

As at so many megalithic sites in Western Europe, the Goddess symbolism forms the core of the constructional plan. At Lepenski Vir, the Irish court tombs and elsewhere Marija Gimbutas interpreted the forward extension of stone settings as the Goddess's open legs, and the crescent-shaped forecourts of the Severn-Cotswold barrows could well hint at this, too. This architectural trick appears at the long barrow sites known as Hetty Pegler's Tump, Notgrove and Nympsfield (all in Gloucestershire) besides Stoney Littleton. Long barrows in the Cotswold Hills at Cherington (Avening), Rodmarton and Nempnett Thrubwell in Avon County (and probably too at Lanhill (Wiltshire) and Belas Knap) had port-holed megaliths in them which physically complement the symbolism of the womb opening. The effect was produced by cutting half-circles in two adjacent slabs, except at Nempnett Thrubwell (now destroyed) where a single slab was perforated.

Lepenski Vir was clearly a shrine. So are they all. And many were temples too, functioning as churches of the Goddess, although receiving bones of the dead as did European Christian churches and cathedrals. The barrows facing the

The constricted openings of some long barrows are plainly identifiable as the Goddess's womb opening. This sketch was made in 1809 by J. Burden in Avening, Gloucestershire, soon after the stone chambers of a barrow had been taken there following total excavation by the vicar. Leslie Grinsell suggests that the destroyed barrow was at Cherington a few kilometres away.

midwinter sunrise received the light of the New Year. Those facing east, as at West Kennet near Avebury, celebrated the equinoxes. Others, as at East Kennet, faced north-east—the midsummer sunrise. What spiritual reasoning drove the Neolithic peoples to create these alignments?

Timothy Darvill has summarised the radiocarbon dating evidence for the Cotswold-Severn chambered barrows. 'From the radiocarbon dates it is clear that the tombs were being built by about 3100 b.c. or about 3800 calendar years BC, and it can be suggested that a starting date even earlier would not be unreasonable.' The megalithic phase of the Wayland's Smithy barrow in West Oxfordshire has characteristics in common with the Stoney Littleton barrow, including fossil-bearing dry-stone walling imported a distance of 65 kilometres from the geological neighbourhood of Stoney Littleton. The single known radiocarbon date for Wayland's Smithy, indicating about 3500 BC (2820±130 b.c.), comes from material which only shortly antedated the chambering of the barrow. Radiocarbon dating at the earthen long barrow at Nutbane (Hampshire) points to about 3400 BC (2730±150 b.c.)

These dates confirm that for many centuries before the founding of the first Stonehenge (about 3200 BC), to say nothing of later Silbury Hill and Avebury, and at the time of the fourth-millennium BC causewayed enclosures like Windmill Hill and Robin Hood's Ball, a religion of the Great Goddess was prevalent and all-powerful.

Just how widespread was solar orientation of Stone Age Goddess monuments? A look at some supreme examples from other parts of Britain and Ireland will give an idea of its popularity.

On the island of Anglesey there is a round tumulus with stone-lined passage and internal chamber in which is located a free-standing megalith called the pillar stone. This is the famous Bryn Celli Dhu monument. The name 'pillar stone' was possibly selected by last century's excavators as a euphemism for 'betyl' or phallus, but the stone is more likely to be a Goddess Stone than a phallic one. My view is that this megalith, as well as hundreds of others in Britain and Brittany which are generally looked upon as phallic, represented in part the integration of the sexes—that is, of the deities. In other words, in the symbolic reality of the time the stone stood for the generating power of the universe. As a holy megalith, it was at one and the same time a Goddess Stone, a life-force symbol, and perhaps pseudo-phallic as well. This menhir, like so many others, was a Goddess icon, a cult stone of the Age of the Goddess.

At Bryn Celli Dhu the slab-walled gallery pointed north-east, permitting internal illumination only about the time of midsummer sunrise. At this period of the year the energy of the sun would flood in, illuminating the chamber with direct and reflected light, although without direct light striking the Goddess Stone.

External view of Bryn Celli Dhu on the island of Anglesey. This Goddess temple
has several design elements which demonstrate a strongly-developed belief in
the world of the Goddess.

In the court cairn tombs of Ireland at Ballymarlagh, County Antrim, and at
Deer Park, County Sligo, the passages with their Goddess 'legs' are open to the
south-east; at Shanballyemond, County Tipperary, and Clady Haliday, County
Tyrone, the direction is north-east, and at Ballyglass, County Mayo, it is
north-west.

The religious imagery of the unrivalled temples of Newgrange and Knowth is
explained in *The Goddess of the Stones*. The huge mound of Knowth is penetrated by two long gallery-passages, one from the east, the other from the west.
At Newgrange the direction is south-east, and corresponds precisely with that
of the rising midwinter sun. Megaliths stand outside the tumuli in line with the
passages. Exactly what is the spiritual meaning of solar alignments? What mystical philosophy lay behind the physical reality of the sun radiating heat and light
into the depths of a womb-temple?

The splendid menhir at Dol, typical of the great standing stones of Brittany.
Such stones were at the focus of a cult of the Goddess and some are
carved with Goddess features or insignia.

4

The Marriage of the Gods

For thousands of years, during the Palaeolithic and Neolithic Ages, the Goddess was universally adored. She *was* the universe: Life-giver and Life-taker, source of luxuriance and fruitfulness, and the recipient of the dead who were born again from her womb. Many early creation myths start with a Universal Mother who at some stage generates by self-reproduction, or by marriage with a convenient god, a line of descent which leads ultimately to human beings on earth. Mircea Eliade held that the creation myth provided a model and justification for all human activities, besides standing as the archetype of a community's set of myths and rituals. He believed that every idea of renewal, or of beginning again, is traceable to the notion of 'birth' which, in its turn, goes back to the doctrine of the 'birth' of the cosmos.

A common element in creation myths and annual rituals celebrating the renewal of the world was the Cosmic Marriage or Sacred Marriage—the union of the deities—which assured the everlasting process of creation and the continuance of the universe. Most obvious were the celestial marriages, those between the deities representing Heaven and Earth, or Sun and Moon. In Tahiti, as H. M. Westropp and C. S. Wake recorded in 1875, 'it was supposed that the sun and moon, which are gods, had begotten the stars, and the eclipses were the time of their copulation'. Mircea Eliade commented that the marriage of Heaven and Earth was 'often thought of in quite literal terms, *ut maritus supra feminam in coitione iacet, sic coelum supra terram.*' (As the husband lies above his wife in sexual union, so the sky covers the earth.) It is surely no coincidence that in European languages the sky is often masculine and earth feminine, the sun masculine and moon feminine. It is of course dangerous to generalise, for in some pre-Christian and pre-Islamic cultures, as in Japan, the sun was a Goddess. In Celtic Britain the feminine sun was called Sol or Sul at the time that the Romans arrived, and rites were observed on hilltops overlooking springs. In the Roman city of *Aquae Sulis* (Bath), joint altars were raised with the Roman Goddess Minerva under the name Sul Minerva. One of Bath's hills is called Solsbury Hill, after the same Goddess.

Although by Celtic times the once mighty Neolithic Goddess had been relegated to the subordinate role of Earth Mother or Great Mother and was serving as a consort to a higher male god, the Irish and Welsh kings still ceremonially married the local Goddess. Miranda Green writes that the council members or elders of a tribe acted as governors for a divine figure or queen, who personified the Great Mother and presided over a matrilineal society. The King reigned, not in his own right, but because he was the consort of the Divine Woman.

This rite of Sacred or Divine Marriage as applied to Celtic or Iron Age royal weddings was a degenerate form of an ancient tradition, but it hints at the character of the underlying mythology even if we cannot recover precise details. For the many people working on the land the paramount need for fertile soil ensured that the old ideas persisted in agricultural societies for hundreds of years longer, and to a small extent survived the greatest onslaught of all, that of Christianising reform in the first millennium AD. In her book *Gods and Myths of Northern Europe* H. R. Ellis Davidson quotes from a poetic fertility charm dating from the Anglo-Saxon era. With a degree of Christian editing the Church allowed the substance of the old planting rite and lengthy invocation to remain. Within this, the evergreen ritual of the annual marriage between Heaven and Earth shines through brightly. For the ceremony, the wood of the plough was anointed with incense, fennel, consecrated soap and salt, and the seed for planting was placed upon it too. Then came the sacred appeal:

> Erce, Erce, Erce, Earth Mother,
> may the Almighty Eternal Lord
> grant you fields to increase and flourish,
> fields fruitful and healthy,
> shining harvest of shafts of millet,
> broad harvests of barley . . .
> Hail to thee, Earth, Mother of Men!

Bring forth now in God's embrace,
filled with good for the use of men.

This remnant is a precious memory from a vanished age. Similar appeals lived on in Neolithic America, Africa and Asia right into the present century, but in Europe, a thousand years ago, time was running out with the intensifying persecution of what little remained of the once sovereign Great Goddess, Mistress of all Nature and Peoples of the Earth.

So what can we learn of the Ritual Marriage in its formative days, thousands of years before the British Saxon period? The answers exist, engraved on cave walls, rocks and megaliths waiting to be deciphered, and they live on in the construction of the monuments, too. It is a matter of seeking the clues and establishing their meanings. If we look back at the Upper Palaeolithic period and then the Neolithic, we shall find time and time again the plainest evidence of the Sacred Marriage myth, the Marriage of the Gods.

One such image was found carved on reindeer bone at Laugerie Basse in the Dordogne, except that the male we see here is not human. This telling picture,

Carving on reindeer bone, about 15,000 years old, from Laugerie Basse in the Dordogne. It is likely that the carving represents the Divine Marriage between the Great Goddess and her God.

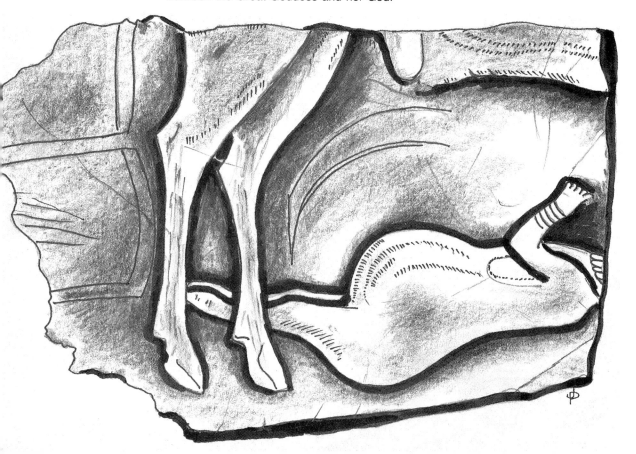

dating from the middle Magdalenian period, around 12000 BC, has been ill understood by most observers. Alexander Marschak has come nearest to providing an
acceptable explanation. The legs and phallus of a bull bison are seen high above
a pregnant woman lying on her back, and Marschak suggests that the scene
formed part of a ritual in which a woman and an animal told a story about the
Goddess and a mythical animal, symbolic of the life-renewing force and perhaps
intended to ensure human fertility, earth fertility or an abundance of hunting
animals. What is more probable in my view is that the virile bison is an animal
manifestation of some male god, a consort for the Goddess, whose phallic power
arrives from above as if from the heavens or the clouds. In other words, the
scene really portrays the active relationship between the fertile deities, a form
of Sacred Marriage, and is a plea for fruitfulness at the human level. Cut on
bone the image was portable, hand-size; it could be clasped by a woman in
childbirth.

An even earlier representation of the joining of male and female principles
appears in a simple engraving from Isturitz in the French Pyrenees. Phallus and
vulva come together in union: a harmonious blend of the life-giving principles
in partnership, the earliest known rendering of what may be the Sacred Marriage.
Its age is judged to be 21000–20000 BC. The deities are reduced to their essential
attributes, which leads to an extraordinary simplicity and economy of design.

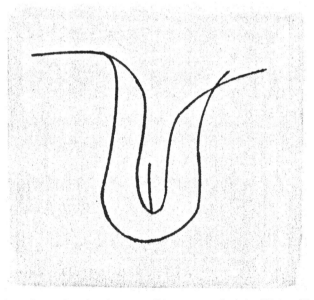

Phallus and vulva in union—the simplest possible portrayal of the Divine Marriage or Sacred
Marriage theme. Stone engraving from Isturitz in the French Pyrenees.

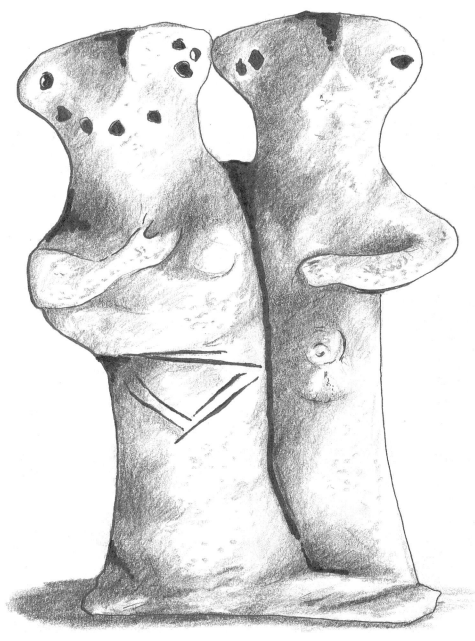

Clay statuette from Cascioarele in south-eastern Europe. Because the figures are masked, they may represent a dramatic portrayal of a Sacred or Divine Marriage. Dated at 6500 BC or earlier.

During the long epoch of cave painting and statuary manufacture in central and southern Europe much of Britain and Ireland was under ice and uninhabited. Not until the Mesolithic Age did hunters return across the land bridge from the Continent into Britain, and then around 8000 BC the bridge was ruptured as rising sea levels created the Straits of Dover. On the Continent, in the course of time, the agricultural age arrived and the well-established Palaeolithic Goddess became the Neolithic Goddess. A major centre of the agrarian revolution was Anatolia, now Turkey, from the heart of which, at Catal Hüyük, comes the earliest recognisable rendering between human likenesses of what appears to be the Sacred Marriage. The date is about 5750 BC. It is a sculpture in relief with four images, which the excavator James Mellaart described as two deities embracing and, on their right, a mother with a child. Mellaart wondered whether these scenes might portray consecutive events: sexual union followed by the successful delivery of a son. He commented: 'The Goddess remains the same, the male appears either as husband or son. This may be one of the earliest representations of the *hieros gamos*, the Sacred Marriage.'

A fifth-millennium Balkan statuette from Cascioarele showing another bridal pair could also be connected with the Sacred Marriage ritual. As Marija Gimbutas remarks in *Goddesses and Gods of Old Europe*, the masked figures suggest an annual event at which a wedding ceremony is enacted and the Great Goddess marries a potent god.

All the concepts of the Goddess religion would have been carried into Britain by the migrating hunters. Later, in the fifth millennium BC, the first agricultural-ists would have arrived not only with their planting and husbandry techniques, but with an agrarian version of the Neolithic Goddess and her myths and symbols. A fourth-millennium occupation site and ritual centre in Dorset contains the oldest known mural in England: an outline drawing scratched into the side of a chalk-cut trench on the outskirts of the county town of Dorchester, the design restating the message from Isturitz. Sublime in its simplicity, it focuses on the essential function of the Sacred Marriage—consummation. It confirms that in Southern England around 3500 BC the ritual impregnation of the Goddess was already an essential part of the spiritual fabric of the age.

Long before I knew of this mural (it was only discovered in 1987) I had already arrived at this conclusion, principally by deciphering 'the language of the megaliths'. There are numerous Irish and British megaliths and rock carvings of the fourth and third millennia which abound in cryptic engravings—spirals, lozenges, zigzags. They provide a symbolic legacy of religious ideas from the past which are a challenge to our curiosity. The symbols are not the random jottings of an idle peasantry but the deliberate carvings of a pious people and ruling priest-class. I have found that left-handed spirals generally denote feminin-

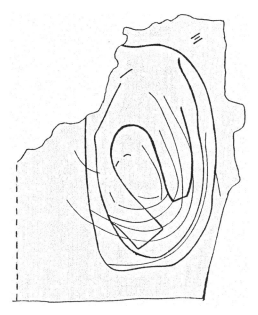

Drawing found on the subterranean wall of a chalk ditch at Dorchester in 1987. The theme is again that of the Sacred Marriage of the Gods.

ity and the Goddess; right-handed spirals stand for masculinity and a male deity or consort. Outward-flowing spirals equate with birth, growth and rebirth; inward-flowing spirals designate death and destruction. Once we know this, and the meanings of lozenges, triangles, zigzags, circles and cups, we can understand simple stories and statements about lunar and solar movements which are engraved on specific stones. The theme of Sacred Marriage recurs frequently in messages stored for thousands of years, their meaning concealed until now.

The joining of unlike spirals produces a scroll-like coil. It is found on door lintels, rock carvings, and standing stones. In it we see a Holy Marriage of the Goddess whose consummation guarantees the fertility of the Earth. It is an artistic statement of the life-generating union of sexual opposites which, by their marriage, sets the divine cycle in motion. The symbol can be seen on stones and rocks which were carved in Britain and Ireland in the fourth and third millennia BC, and throughout the Neolithic stages of all the other continents of the world. Because it is found on surviving artefacts of ceramic, wood, metal and bone from many other countries too, it is likely that the returning spiral, like the plain spiral, had the same high spiritual significance whenever it was included as a design element on cloth and tapestry, baskets and other perishable objects,

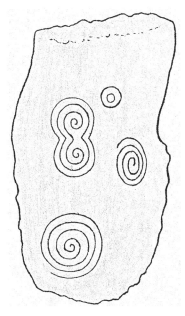

Megalithic engravings showing separate left-hand and right-hand Goddess and Sky God spirals and also a pair joined as if in marriage. This example is from the Calderstones, Liverpool.

suggesting that they were used for sacred purposes. In other religions at other times various images were conjured up to symbolise these same ideas. In Egypt the 'sma amulet' was a sexual union design which incorporated the essential elements of the Divine Marriage. In Hindu India the Tantric altar-stone performed the same function for the primary deities. In China the Yang and the Yin featured a similar concept concerning the natural union of opposites. And in Western Europe the Neolithic mace, like the pestle and mortar, was a religious symbol of authority on account of its male-female integration within a Divine Marriage context.

There are two other ways in which unlike spirals may come together in sacred matrimony. An engraving from the Neolithic Age of Nias, an island west of Sumatra, was spotted by F. M. Schnitger on a stone *niogaji* at Tetegewo. A *niogaji* is a mushroom-shaped stone always dedicated to a woman, in contrast to the pillar stone (a *behu*) which is a monument to a man. They are usually a metre high and 0.6 to two metres in diameter, and very often the *behu* and the *niogaji* stand next to one another. The base of the *niogaji* is a short pillar which widens into an arching section with a flat upper surface. On ceremonial occasions prominent wives dance on the female stones which emit a musical tone when struck firmly by hand or foot. Schnitger stresses that the incised decoration underneath is not readily visible. 'One wonders what the real purpose of these ogive decorations is, for, unless one bends down, they are practically invisible. It is possible that they were not made to please the eye but in order to attract some magical power'.

The paired-spiral images and the tail-to-tail lizards seem to be variants on the Sacred Marriage theme. The lizards are animal aspects of a deity, for images of divine lizards bearing special powers are relatively abundant in Indonesia. The chief's house in Orahil, Nias, has a wooden carving of a woman mated with a lizard which, in the context of a specialised mythology, denoted the union of two deities. The stone shows the lizard-God and lizard-Goddess preparing to mate tail to tail, and this is repeated by their spiral equivalents depicted in conjugal union and opposition. Less certain is the meaning of the triangles, but since Sumatra retains a traditional matrilineal society to this day, the typically-female triangles could represent volcanic cones with vaginal entrances to the womb of the earth. Certainly, much of the symbolism from the world's Neolithic ages, especially that related to the Goddess, is universally recognisable and examples can be found everywhere. The less-common spiral juxtaposition in the Nias engraving is not unique to Indonesia. It has been found in Britain in combination with the lozenge shape, engraved on one of three devotional objects of chalk known as the Folkton drums, unearthed from a round barrow near Folkton in Yorkshire. What significance does the lozenge design have, since it occurs so frequently in Neolithic and Bronze Age art?

There are several Neolithic megaliths in obviously holy places which bear the three–spiral design, such as Newgrange in Ireland, where all three spirals are

Opposing spirals and other motifs combine artistically in these Indonesian megalithic engravings to produce a message that was not normally intended to be seen. Because lizards and spirals in Nias, Sumatra, stood for deities, the message is again that of the Sacred Divine Marriage.

left-handed, feminine spirals. The meaning is that of the tri-function Goddess. In other engravings, one or more of the three spirals are replaced by lozenges, so that the lozenge and the left-handed spiral both appear to be Goddess equivalents—emblems of august divinity. The lozenge shape, apparently—as well as other symbols mentioned in the previous chapter—is nothing but a representation of the Sacred Vulva. Its shape is not unlike the appearance of the labia at the time of giving birth. This quintessential female attribute identifies the lozenge as a symbol of the life-giving, child-bearing Goddess. In time it came to signify the Goddess herself, and must have been recognised throughout Britain and Ireland as her symbol. Being much easier to develop into design motifs than the coiling spiral, it became extremely popular, and appeared on artefacts everywhere in Europe, including the Stonehenge region.

A symbol which is fundamentally different in meaning but highly significant to an understanding of prehistoric culture is the circle. In Neolithic Britain this shape appeared everywhere in the form of stone circles, circular earthen-bank enclosures, henges, round barrows and round houses. At the stone-carving level it has been found as hand-size circles or cup-shaped depressions with or without concentric rings. Its chief significance was as sacred space marked out by the raising of a circular bank, or a ring of stones or timber, around a centre. The perimeter created, at least symbolically, a boundary between the sacred and the secular. The circle was the shape of the distant horizon, beyond which lay another world, chaotic, unknown and potentially unsafe, where strangers lived. On a smaller scale the sacred stone circle mirrored the cosmic circle, by enclosing an area of security where communication could take place with the Goddess.

In the middle was the Centre of the World, which was seen to be on the world axis joining the centre of the subterranean world with the zenith of the sky. On ceremonial occasions the most holy object or person would have been at the centre, or close to it. In some stone circles a selected megalith had the place of honour, as in the middle and late periods of Stonehenge when the so-called Altar Stone stood practically at the circle centre. In the first phase of Stonehenge a wooden building or timber ring occupied the entire central area, 30–31 metres in diameter.

All these sacred circles, whether of stone, wood or earth, were used for ceremonial and festive purposes. Burials took place at times, and rites and worship at these times and others. But there is also evidence of their use for happier, although still solemn, occasions, some of which related to fertility rites.

Why in Britain did it happen that there was such an explosion of interest in the *round* monument from the last quarter of the fourth millennium onwards? I have discussed this at length in *The Goddess of the Stones*, but briefly, I believe there is a link between the round marks made naturally in fields by atmospheric

A naturally-formed crop-circle with an outward-flowing spiral issuing from an obvious centre, found in a wheatfield in southern England. In round barrow burials bodies were curved into a foetal shape at the supposed womb-opening of the Goddess circle, as shown here.

vortices and the raising of these monuments. Scientists are agreed that, as a result of atmospheric-vortex action, plain circular marks and rings have always affected British fields, and particularly those in central southern England, notably Wessex, the home of Stonehenge, Avebury, Stanton Drew, Woodhenge, and many thousands of round barrows and timber rings besides.

The circular vortex marks were viewed as a sacred manifestation of the Goddess. The spiral centre was taken to correspond to her vulva and the area was marked out as a sanctuary. Because such circles seemed highly desirable places in which to deposit the dead, a round barrow tradition began and spread all over Britain. For people desiring immortality, the attraction of burial at the spiral centre, the Goddess's womb-opening, must have been irresistible. The Age of Stonehenge came to be typified by the Goddess circle, appearing everywhere in the monumental and barrow designs, while the spiral and the lozenge took pre-eminence as the cult symbols of the age.

As for the cup, this device was also related to the vulva and aimed largely in the direction of spirits. The cup in the rock allowed spirits to pass—those of the ancestors and those from the Goddess—and so permitted a degree of communication with the Goddess and the ancestors. Some cup-marks were made to let 'fertilising' solar energy pass through, while others played a direct role in fertility rituals. The cup-and-ring marks, so common in Northern Britain, had a practical, highly specialised role—to release a spirit into the womb of a pregnant or barren woman in order to animate the baby prior to a safe delivery.

The ultimate in Goddess worship, as regards the earth-moving capabilities of the Neolithic population in Britain, was the building of Silbury Hill. This enormous mound was built to honour the Great Goddess and to allow ceremonies to be performed on the summit directly above the inner turf core and its hidden circles. The Goddess was central to the life and well-being of the age: omniscient, omnipresent, and the basis of the unity of all Nature. As Marija Gimbutas said in *The Language of the Goddess*, 'Her power was in water and stone, in tomb and cave, in animals and birds, snakes and fish, hills, trees, and flowers.'

In the prehistoric world symbolism provided potent visual imagery to help the believer and worshipper understand the mythology and the religion of his or her tribe, and make sense of the mysteries of life, death and the universe. Such beliefs answered the chief questions raised by the early farmers: what were the origins of the seasons, of plant renewal, of animal and human birth? How could the resurrection of the world be assured—annually for the seasons, and after death for humanity? The Goddess religion must have provided satisfactory answers because it endured as a religion of comparative peace for the greater part of the prehistory of humankind.

1. The Venus of Laussel. The oldest known human sculpture carved to convey
a tangible message, she forms part of a Palaeolithic frieze at a cave entrance in southern
France. In her right hand she holds a cornucopia.

2. Swallowhead spring, whose waters feed the River Kennet, formerly known
locally as the Cunnit or Cunnt.

3. La Gran'mère du Castel, a splendid Goddess icon from Neolithic Guernsey. She has clearly
carved shoulders and breasts, and wears a necklace. *Photo June Peel*

4. Artistically portrayed vulvar symbolism on stone R9 in the Goddess temple at Gavrinis,
off the Breton coast. The power of the holy images is overwhelming and moving.

5. Stoney Littleton long barrow, near Bath, Avon. Deep inside the passage the midwinter sun touches the cup-like pit of the slab in chamber C. Nowadays, an unplanned bulge in the gallery wall prevents full penetration of light.

6. Stoney Littleton. From inside the passage, the rising full moon is framed in the vulvar doorway. Its light strikes an ammonite fossil on a slab at the entrance to chamber G.

5

The Sky God Mates with Earth

In all the surviving mythologies that have reached us from Stone Age societies there is a deep-rooted fascination with the origins of life and the universe. The myths explained and thereby validated—because they were held to be the absolute truth—the creation of the sun, the moon and the stars, the origins of animal and vegetable life, and the emergence of human ancestors. Just as importantly, tribal mythologies helped to give meaning to death by justifying people's beliefs in a paradise beyond the grave.

As the sacred history of the community, myths formed the basis of social life and culture, lying at the foundation of spiritual beliefs. Human psyche has changed but little since, although values and perceptions have, and later religions encountered similar problems in coming to terms with the genesis of life.

In the earliest stages of spiritual thought, from its beginnings in the Palaeolithic Age, religions were relatively simple, based on a supreme deity who in Europe was usually a Great Goddess but in certain regions and among some tribes in other continents was a divinity of indeterminate sex. In the Neolithic Age, as dependence on a farming economy developed, the power of the Earth Goddess grew within the domain of the Great Goddess; the concept of a union between Earth and Sky was universal, although initially the Sky God was altogether inferior in importance. The farmers of the Neolithic and Bronze Ages prayed to the Goddess and her male consorts to make the world fertile, joyful and intelligible, to bestow moderate weather conditions and a regularity in the changing seasons. And everywhere that farmers took their religion, symbol and image went too. Although people were illiterate, they knew how to express their main beliefs and prayers in pictorial code—on pots and on stones and rocks.

The realms of the Great Goddess were Moon, Heaven, Earth and Waters—she was an all-powerful divinity of fertility who incorporated within herself the agrarian duties of Earth Mother. Only much later did an Earth Goddess separate out as a fully fecund deity around whom rather elaborate agricultural cults evolved, some of which filtered down into our own era. In the simpler myths of the Earlier Neolithic period the consort of the Great Goddess was the less dominant yet vigorously male Sky God, and in Britain there is evidence that he acquired a degree of importance quite early on—probably as early as the middle of the fourth millennium BC.

Wherever a Sky God was recognised, he was held responsible for the elements and vagaries of the cloud-bearing atmosphere. These natural phenomena are comprehensible to us because we have the benefit of scientific explanations and the received wisdom of philosophical traditions, but in early times the agencies of nature were seen as terrible and awesome manifestations of the sacred. Above all else, the Sky God displayed his might in the thunderstorm, and for this he was respected because of his prodigious powers of destruction and his ability to make the soil fruitful through his gift of life-giving rain. Only later did he develop into a Storm God proper with his own highly developed cult.

As a Sky God he was the thrower of lightning-bolts and the slinger of hailstones. He announced himself with a thunderous voice likened to the roar of a bull; lightning illuminated the thunderhead and bolts shrieked to the ground, striking trees and animals and people. This was his terrible side; he was then the vengeance seeker, exacting punishment for some offence committed by the community, and occasionally called upon to bring destruction to the enemy. We know this through countless parallels from New Stone Age societies elsewhere, which provide overwhelming proof that from the time of Neolithic Asia and Europe onwards the thunderbolt, the axe and the bull were symbols closely connected with the atmospheric deities. Indeed, because of the much-studied religions of Eastern Europe we know how persistent these concepts were, and that they recognisably lasted through the Bronze and Iron Ages, through Mycenae and Crete, and into Classical Greece and Rome.

For stock-farmers the bull was the mightiest of the domesticated animals. They were keenly aware of his prodigious strength and of the instrument of his fertile potency. Consequently, because the thunderstorm sounded like a bull and behaved like one, the Sky God was personified as a bull or its image in the earthly rites of worship and sacrifice. At the same time the Goddess revealed her interest in the bull-cult through the horns which she displayed in her lunar manifestation. By their very shape bull's horns evoked the symbolism of the uterus, which has led Marija Gimbutas and others to suggest that the bull's head and horns displayed in a ritual context—known as the bucranium—came to stand for regeneration, representing the reproductive womb of the Goddess. Perhaps because they also created an opportunity to eat the meat, sacrificial cults and feasts evolved, and in later times, if not earlier, the head of a slain bull was offered to the celestial God and its blood to the terrestrial side of the Goddess. Remnants of ceremonial sacrifice within the prehistoric bull-cult survive to this day, for instance in the bull fights of Spain and southern France.

The cult of the bull became widespread early in the Mediterranean Neolithic period, and certainly extended into the spiritual thought of the British Neolithic people, having been conveyed there at the time of the ancestral migrations which brought the first corn, pots and domesticated animals. Considerable evidence for the cult has been found from Neolithic and Bronze Age excavation sites, starting with foundation and funerary offerings in fourth-millennium ritual enclosures and long barrows. The rites included offerings of bulls' heads, at times with feet and other body parts of which only the white bones remain. A good example of a bucranium of *Bos primigenius* came from the infill of the fourth-millennium bank barrow inside Maiden Castle, and other big-horned skulls from Neolithic Dorset are now in the County Museum. The smaller *Bos longifrons* did not reach Britain until much later, at the time of the Beaker people.

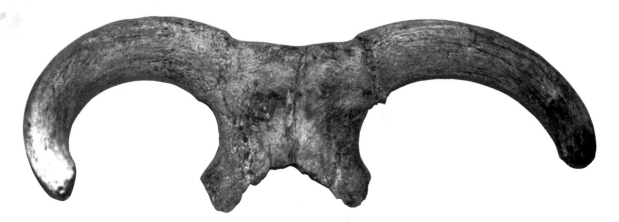

Bull's horns from a Neolithic Dorset monument. *Photo courtesy of the Dorset Natural History and Archaeological Society, Dorset County Museum, Dorchester*

There is another side to celestial potency, greater by far than any force that the ordinary thunderstorm can unleash. This is the tornadic whirlwind, which created such a wondrous yet alarming revelation as to imprint tribal tales with accounts that must have dominated mythological traditions for ever more.

The whirling winds of the tornado descend from the thunderstorm as a spinning funnel of cloud and roaring wind. For tense minutes the tornado pursues a straight or winding trail over hill and dale. Terrifying forces are unleashed. Everything in its path is at risk: life, property, crops and trees. A swathe is cut through woods, a scar is left in fields; yet all the while the range of intense winds is localised, and a short distance beyond the limits of the path of devastation there is little or no damage. For the beholder it is an awe-inspiring sight. An appendage like that of the strongest bull has swooped to the ground and made union with Earth. Witnesses liken the roar of a tornado to the noise of a thousand bulls—why not indeed? The tornado is the Celestial Bull, the primordial Taurus himself. In this role the Sky God has descended to the farmer's habitat; he has united with the Goddess, and track and traces remain as witnesses. The world of a Goddess-worshipping, agricultural community has seen the Sky meet Earth. The community has been blessed with the majesty of a Cosmic Consummation.

To the Neolithic people it would be an act of creation, a Marriage of the Gods which maintains and revitalises the universe. The spiralling tornado funnel, sweeping field and forest in the thunderstorm, arrives at the peak of the storm. In hurried intromission a searing gash is cut across the countryside. But the climax passes, the roar recedes, and the air falls still. Spectators are dumbfounded. An event of cosmic significance has taken place on Earth, and been perceived as the glorious entry of the Bull God into the Goddess's body. The tornado track is an undeniable testament to a Sacred Consummation between the divinities of Sky and Earth.

The theme of Sacred Marriage not only appears throughout the mythology of the ancient world, it continues into the well-documented classical period as well, and frequently makes use of allusions to intercourse between a Thunder God and Earth Goddess, at times noble and tender, at others raw and ravishing. This quotation is from the Greek Aeschylus who lived from 525 to 456 BC:

> The holy Heaven doth live to wed the ground,
> And Earth conceives a love of marriage,
> The rain that falls from husband Heaven
> Impregnates Earth; and she for mortal men gives birth
> To pastoral herbage and to Ceres' corn.

Another rendering declares 'the holy Sky is intoxicated with desire from penetrating the body of Earth'. Just as relevant is the union of Aeneas and Dido as told by Virgil (70–19 BC) in *The Aeneid*, for a storm erupts while the pair consummate their union. The epic relates that the nymphs are weeping on the heights of the mountains as the thunder crashes and the lightning flashes, signifying that the God of Heaven is approaching his marriage partner, the Earth Mother.

The myth of the 'creative storm' is universal throughout the post-Neolithic Indo-European period and every culture has its own weather divinity. The Storm God of the Hittites wields an axe in his right hand and holds an object representing lightning, or less likely a tree, in his left. His long hair flows half-way

Two axe-wielding Storm Gods from the second millennium Indo-European era of the Middle East. *Left*: a Hittite God from Zinjirli; *right*: Baal from Ras Shamra, Ugarit. Because Baal has a lightning spear in his left hand, the Hittite God too is probably grasping a clutch of lightning bolts or their symbolic equivalent, which is an early version of the trident suggesting a male trinity.

down his back, ending in a spiral. The phallic shape of his cap may symbolise and augment his abilities to influence fertility. The axe-bearing storm god Baal from Ugarit, as portrayed on a relief from Ras Shamra, more powerfully features the pointed cap and spiralling hair, his most daunting tornadic features.

Another splendid representation of the Bull God or Storm God came from Jokha (ancient Umma, of Mesopotamia). The bull's horns, the tail and what may be hooves, combined with the erect phallus and spiralling hair, resulted in

The Bull-God from Jokha in ancient Umma, Mesopotamia. The spiralling hair, horns and erect phallus combine to create a formidable fertility god at a time when male gods were rising to prominence in the post-Goddess Indo-European era.

the figure of a commanding weather god, Lord of the Thunderstorm and the Tornado.

The pre-Iron Age inhabitants of the British islands have left us with no similar images of male deities (perhaps like the American Indians they fashioned their gods in perishable wood instead of immutable stone or ceramic, or perhaps there was a taboo on human images) but these anthropomorphic impressions from other cultures give some idea of how the British Neolithic people may have visualised their Sky God.

One clue we have closer to home is the English chalk carving, 55 metres tall, cut into the side of a steep hill at Cerne Abbas in Dorset. Although its origins are obscure, the style of its outline and the conspicuous emblems of fertility suggest a date no later than Romano-British, and it could have been cut and re-cut from an earlier figure dating from the first-millennium Iron Age. Despite being much later than the deities of the Neolithic era, it is a good example of divine masculine potency, shown as strength in arm and virility, the instinctive attributes of an agrarian society's god; clearly it descends in spirit from the beliefs of earlier ages. It may be no accident that this image is associated with a prehistoric earthwork within which maypole rituals were maintained for hundreds of years, and well into the present century—The Trendle or 'Frying Pan', or possibly 'dripping pan' as Paul Newman pointed out in *Gods and Graven Images*. He added that in country parlance the name alludes to the female sexual

The huge chalk-hill carving of a prehistoric British god at Cerne Abbas, Dorset. The earthwork known as the Trendle is on the crest of the hill above him.

organ, which explains the name Frying Pan and the spring fertility rites held there. Similar reasoning might explain the name of the Neolithic spiral-causewayed site near Goodwood, Sussex, known as the Trundle. Folk memories can be long, and the origins of some names are thought to reach back to the Bronze Age and even the Neolithic. The belief that barren women would bear children after sleeping on the giant's phallus could have originated from a desire for impregnation by the soul-spirit.

Everything that descends from the heavens is sacred. This includes rain and hailstones, especially when discharged from a thunderstorm, and above all the funnel cloud or spout. With its whirling, spiralling motion this is the supreme symbol of Heaven, for it is the only element of the atmosphere which returns skywards after descending from Heaven to Earth. The sublime fitness of the vision of withdrawal completes the celestial and divine imagery. The watching believer knows he has witnessed the phallus of a god. The rain was the god's semen, and the lightning and hail were his arms and gifts.

What was the response of the community to this demonstration of celestial power? Interpreting the mating of the Sky God with the Goddess on Earth as an act of creation, their reaction was to prepare immense earthworks by which the area sanctified by celestial descent would be preserved as a permanent record of the tract of land where the Divine Masculine had met the Great Feminine. Today we call these exceptional monuments *cursuses*.

In his thesis on Neolithic cursuses Roy Loveday suggested that 'it is feasible that they were put up to demarcate a sacred area of land dedicated to the gods, a *temenos* or holy precinct'. This conclusion, although not specific as to its origins, nevertheless tallies perfectly with my own findings.

More than fifty cursus monuments are known to have been constructed in Neolithic Britain. They consist of two widely spaced, parallel ditches and banks of very great length which ride the landscape, up and down, often for one or two kilometres and sometimes for much more. At least two cursuses are between 2.5 and 4 kilometres long, and the longest stretches for ten kilometres through the county of Dorset. Besides the spiritual purpose for which the banks were raised, they also had a lesser practical objective. In order to keep such a vast area weedfree and treeless, the banks and ditches could retain animals for perpetual grazing.

As monuments go, most cursuses are hardly exciting to look at. After five thousand years little remains above ground level, and by the eighteenth and nineteenth centuries the banks and ditches of only three were sufficiently obvious to invite excavation, so confirming their discovery. With the exception of the South Dorset cursus discussed in Chapter 7, traces of the others were detected in air photographs by their effect on crop-growth rates. Few people other than

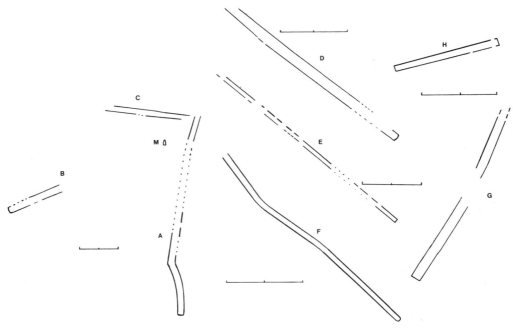

Eight of Britain's cursus monuments. The scales are drawn for 500 metres with subdivisions at 250 metres. On the left are Rudston A, Rudston B, and Rudston C in their correct positions relative to the Rudston Monolith M which is Britain's tallest standing stone at 7.8 metres. The other cursuses are (D) Dorchester-on-Thames (Oxfordshire), (E) Scorton (Yorkshire), (F) Fornham All Saints (Suffolk), (G) Drayton (Oxfordshire) and (H) Springfield (Essex).

archaeologists and antiquarians visit even the best known cursuses, but these puzzling earthworks conceal some very odd and extremely profound secrets indeed.

The reason for their construction has been a deep mystery ever since the observant William Stukeley, when walking near Stonehenge in August 1723, became aware of the importance of the 2700-metre length of parallel shallow ditches which pass from west to east less than a kilometre north of the famous monument. The ditches are about a hundred metres apart, the spoil from each thrown inwards to make low banks of what were once white, but soon grass-covered, chalk rubble. Stukeley recognised the antiquity of these features and imaginatively proposed that the construction had formed a hippodrome or running track which he called a *cursus*, designed for the 'games, feasts, exercises and sports' of the ancient 'holy days'.

No full excavation has been undertaken of the Stonehenge Cursus. There have been some exploratory digs with limited objectives, but additional probing and

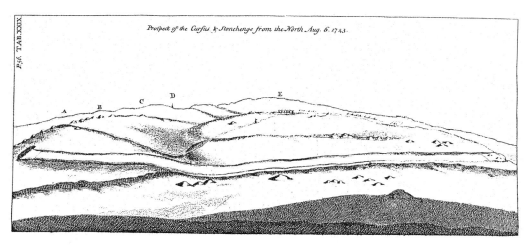

William Stukeley's sketch of the Stonehenge Cursus with Stonehenge (E) visible to the south.

surveying have been made of the whole monument. It was found that the flat-bottomed ditches had been prepared by the laborious extraction of the subsurface solid chalk to a depth below turf level of 0.75 metres, and that the overall length, along both sides and including the high-banked terminal sections, was 5.5 kilometres. Man-power estimates by D.W.A. Startin suggest that a work-load of 100,000 man-hours was needed to complete the task.

At the base of the ditch-section excavated by J. F. S. Stone was a fragment of Welsh Prescelly bluestone, about 90 millimetres across. This and other small clues from ditch and bank prove that the cursus was in use at the time when the pre-Beaker people were active at nearby Stonehenge. The ditches of the cursus appeared to have slowly silted up over the centuries, in contrast with the ditches of a possibly unfinished shorter cursus half-a-kilometre to the north, which had been deliberately filled in before any time for silting had elapsed. The small cursus appears to have been abandoned in favour of building the second, although not before a series of antler horns and antler tools had been deposited along the ditch bottoms, an obviously deliberate act that must have had immense ritual significance. The partial excavations of Julian Richards indicate that both cursuses were constructed before the founding of Stonehenge (3200 BC).

The building of a cursus was a tremendous task for a simple society using primitive tools, but it makes sense if we see it as the effusive devotion of an agrarian people for their Goddess. The cursus was more than just a memorial to an exceptional event in their history because, besides marking the site of a Divine Marriage, it could also be regarded as the Goddess's vulva. Either way it symbolised the Goddess herself. To plough the soil is to create a furrow, but to the devout believer every furrow became a vulva which took the seed and nurtured it. Seed-planting worked because of the influence of the Goddess on the furrow-vulva. The plough and the spade were phalluses, and so was the tornado spout.

The majority of cursuses seem to be between one and two kilometres long although the lengths of several remain uncertain because the positions of one or both ends have not been located. Breadths generally range from forty to a hundred metres. This compares with the average path width of British tornadoes, ranging between 47 and 99 metres. Most tornado tracks are shorter than two kilometres, but at first glance many of the longer ones appear shorter than they really are, due to a 'skipping' effect (caused by intermittent ground contact), or to the tornado crossing open fields and leaving the locality altogether. For either reason, and perhaps to limit the amount of digging involved, the majority of cursus tracks, although tornado-derived, are under two kilometres in length.

TABLE I

Tornado and cursus directions compared on an eight-point compass

TORNADO AZIMUTH DATA			CURSUS AZIMUTH DATA		
Azimuth	*Number*	*Per Cent*	*Azimuth*	*Number*	*Per Cent*
E, ESE	0	0	E, ESE	0	0
SE, SSE	5	2	SE, SSE	2	8
S, SSW	37	12	S, SSW	4	16
SW, WSW	140	46	SW, WSW	10	38
W, WNW	90	29.5	W, WNW	7	27
NW, NNW	29	9.5	NW, NNW	3	11
N, NNE	2	0.5	N, NNE	0	0
NE, ENE	2	0.5	NE, ENE	0	0

Table I and the figure on p. 76 give comparative compass directions of 304 British tornado tracks and 26 cursuses. The tornado track directions were assembled using the data bank of the Tornado and Storm Research Organisation.

The cursus directions were collated after studying the relevant archaeological papers and visiting sites. The immediate problem is to decide which terminal of a cursus is the beginning and which the end, although in practice, where both terminals are known, the constructional details and landscape features leave little room for doubt. The Stonehenge Cursus was plainly intended to run from west to east and not contrariwise, and the Dorset Cursus unarguably begins in the south-west and ends in the north-east. Nor is there usually much difficulty when only one terminus is known, but in a few cases neither terminal has yet been located. These cursuses have been assigned westerly-component rather than easterly-component directions or *azimuths*.

As the figure shows, the agreement between tornado and cursus directions is striking.

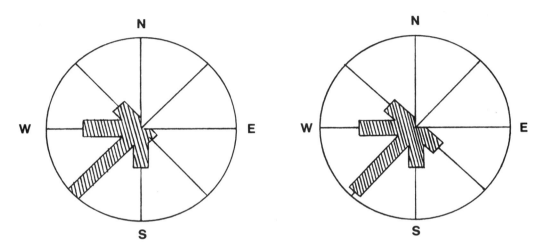

Direction comparisons between tornadoes (*left*) and cursuses (*right*). Most British tornadoes arrive from the south-west (46 per cent) and most cursuses are orientated south-west to north-east (38 per cent).

Although tornadoes are more common in Britain than is generally realised, in any one place they are a rare and unforgettable experience. The horror and astonishment that such an event brings even to a modern community are evident from contemporary accounts of a strong tornado which crossed a sparsely-populated part of Wiltshire in the nineteenth century. The track dimensions, over a landscape of mixed arable and woodland, scale well with those of the Dorset Cursus, and the eye-witnesses expressed their feelings with a sincerity and humility that their Neolithic predecessors might have appreciated.

In 1859, on December 30th, there occurred in Wiltshire, in the vicinity of Calne, an extraordinary tornado, as it was called, or one of those fearful storms which occasionally take place devastating a very narrow track of land, through which the storm cuts a way for itself, levelling trees and all other obstacles that oppose its progress, while the country on either side is left undisturbed. In this instance the length of country traversed was about six miles, the breadth being only 100 to 150 yards. The mighty rush of wind and all the consequent destruction occupied not more than five minutes. Amongst other effects a heavy four-wheeled wagon was taken up and carried completely over a high hedge, and straw and wheat ricks were borne completely away and distributed over the field never to be collected again . . . hundreds of persons came hundreds of miles to visit the district over which the storm had passed.

Three letters about this tornadic whirlwind appeared in *The Times*. One said:

It appeared to have been a regular tornado, having a curvilinear motion, and progressing at a regular rate. Symptoms of an approaching storm were visible at 1 o-clock p.m. The whole atmosphere became thick and heavy. It was so dark that it was scarcely possible to read without artificial light. Presently the vault of heaven was lit up by vivid flashes of lightning, accompanied by loud and sudden claps of thunder, which together with the big hail stones falling thick and fast, and the roaring of the mighty wind, produced a scene at once awful and sublime. The whirlwind seemed to commence on the outskirts of Bowood park . . .

The direction of the track was from west-south-west to east-north-east, the most frequent of tornado directions and the one which happens to be the most common cursus orientation as well. The tornado pursued its path of devastation through the villages of Quemerford, Cherhill, and Yatesbury, a distance of ten kilometres. Beyond this the countryside is more open, for it constitutes the fertile agricultural land and rolling downs that are west, north and north-east of Avebury. Indeed, the tornado funnel must have passed close to the Neolithic causewayed enclosure on Windmill Hill, not far north of the ancient stone avenue west of Avebury. Particulars were given in the *Wiltshire Archaeological Magazine* by the Rev. A. C. Smith, vicar of Yatesbury, whose rectory narrowly escaped harm. He recorded the severe building damage occasioned to Yatesbury and the distant village of Winterbourne Monkton and to isolated farms on Hackpen Hill and near Rockley. The last known mischief, to a few trees, was reported from Ogbourne St George, ten kilometres beyond Yatesbury, the ground-level continuity of the storm being uncertain over this sparsely populated section.

The effect on a modern population, and on the writers, is notable. Describing the vision presented by the tornado the Rev. Mr Smith wrote:

Several persons saw it from a short distance, coming up over the open down, but being on one side of its course, they were entirely out of it, and felt none of its breath as it tore by. Some of these witnesses describe it as a thick volume of smoke, or a dense cloud of steam rushing through the air: but to those within its line, so appalling was its appearance, and so terrific the roar of its approach, that the stoutest heart felt unnerved, and the steadiest head bewildered at so sudden, so unusual, and so fearful a visitation . . . And so sudden and furious was its onset, so loud and deafening its roar, so strange and unearthly the darkness (not unlike that attending the annular eclipse of the sun the previous year), so terrific the crash of falling roofs (tiles and rafters and thatch seeming to fill the air, while the windows were beaten in by the hail), that many thought the Judgment Day had arrived, and others believed an earthquake was demolishing their homes.

The power of the elements impressed the observers of the nineteenth century even as it does today, for tornadoes are infrequent enough and strong enough to justify the attention they get. It is hardly surprising that an archaic community, with no explanation for such a storm, should have seen it as the advent of the Sky God who vaunted his powers while violating and impregnating Earth. So, all those centuries ago, in Neolithic Britain, the cursus was built to commemorate a tornado, that everyone might know of their closeness to the gods. The event would become part of the community's oral mythology, and the descendants would benefit by the cohesion of the group and exclusion of outsiders from knowledge of an historical act identifiable with the time of their ancestors.

Two other points regarding the Wiltshire tornado are important. The first is the giant hail, a common accompaniment to great thunderstorms and tornadoes. As bodies cast out by the Storm God, hailstones would have a highly prized though short-lived life. The fabrication of imitation hailstones in chalk, limestone and other rocks would provide exquisite accessories for the sacramental work of the priest or priestess, and may explain some of the rounded or spherically-shaped rocks whose prehistoric purpose has been regarded as a mystery or else ascribed largely to male fertility matters.

The second point is the date of this tornado, 30 December. It is a fact that British autumns and winters produce more tornadoes than springs and summers. Enthusiasm for cursus construction might be greatest and manpower more readily forthcoming at this low point of the agricultural year.

If the cursus builders wished to celebrate the anniversary of their cosmic visitation, the most effective way of registering the date for all time would be to incorporate a sunrise or sunset alignment within the monument. This I believe

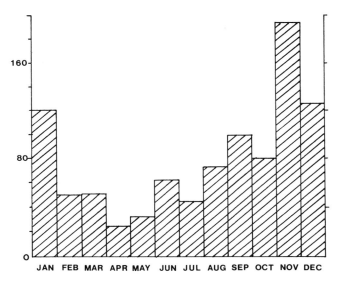

JAN FEB MAR APR MAY JUN JUL AUG SEP OCT NOV DEC

Tornado frequency in Britain according to the month of the year, based on data for the 35 years ending in 1984.

was done for the Dorset Cursus. If it had been done for the Calne tornado, the commemoration date of 30 December would have given a sunrise direction not significantly different from that of the solstice. An alignment to indicate the time of day at which the tornado struck might also have been recorded, so that at the anniversary celebrations the time of occurrence, even perhaps its duration, could be precisely reconstituted.

Examples of strong tornadoes could be multiplied indefinitely. Historical accounts of more than 1,600 British tornadoes, dating back to the eleventh century, are held in the tornado archives of the Tornado and Storm Research Organisation. The following are extracts from eighteenth-century records:

Natural History of Northants, by John Morton
On a Sunday in 1702, there was a Hurricane at Halston that passed on, as it were, in a Glade of 100 yards in Breadth. Within this Space it tore off huge Branches of Trees, twisted a Maple like a Faggot-Band, swept off almost every Tree in John Manning's Orchard in Halston, stript some Houses, and committed other Outrages. It reached from Halston to Northampton . . .

An Account of a Most Terrible Hurricane at Nun-Eaton in Warwickshire, the 29th Augt. 1712, by H. Beighton

It came in the Direction of an Afternoon Azimuth of 42° 30′ The Wind blowing S.W. 6.5¾. Before its reaching Nun-Eaton it came over part of the Parish of Chilvers Coton (where I live) and in its way at the breadth of about 40 or 50 yards Took down all the branches of Trees before it, and where there was much Timber It cut a Perfect Avenue of that Breadth, lopping the trees as exactly as Tho' they had been done by any Gardener for that purpose, nay I saw severall Large Oakes and Elmes where all the Branches were taken clean off on the sides next the Avenue, and Those on the other sides the Trees not broken or interrupted, and where Such Trees Stand full in the Way of the Avenue (As I choose to call it) it either took them up by the Root or cut 'em clean off at or near the Ground, according as The Ground was rising or falling . . .

The passage of the Tornado from Bexhill in Sussex to Newingden, 20th May 1729

The way of the tempest was nearly S. by W. to N. by E. in a direct line, for all variations appeared visibly to be owing and guided by the situation

The phallic funnel of a waterspout coming ashore at Brighton on 21 August 1864.

of the surface of the Earth, always inclining and deflected more or less to the E. or W., in pursuit of the lower ground.

A terrible Whirlwind which happen'd at Corne Abbas in Dorsetshire, Oct. 30. 1731
It began on the South-west Side of the Town, carrying a direct Line to the North-east, crossing the Middle of the Town in Breadth two hundred yards. It stripped and uncovered tiled and thatched Houses, rooted Trees out of the Ground, broke others in the midst of at least a Foot square, and carried the tops a considerable way . . .

What are the characteristics of tornado tracks that make them appear so similar to the outlines of British cursus monuments?

Over level ground tornado tracks normally run in straight lines, or nearly so, and they maintain this regularity across meadow and field, sometimes for kilometres, even over rivers and through forests, so long as the terrain remains comparatively flat. Occasionally the longer tracks may curve gradually, turning slowly either to left or right, remarkably like the Neolithic cursuses illustrated on p.73.

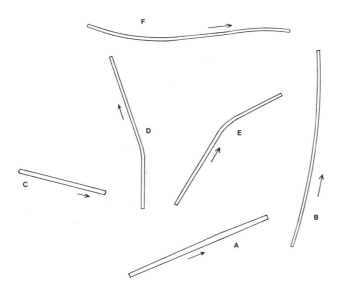

Six British tornado paths illustrating straight tracks and slightly-curving tracks (not drawn to scale). Two examples of kinked paths are included. Lengths vary between half and three kilometres. A: Sussex 1983; B: Berkshire 1979; C: Cambridgeshire 1981; D: Leicestershire 1982; E: Kent 1980; F: Lincolnshire 1982.

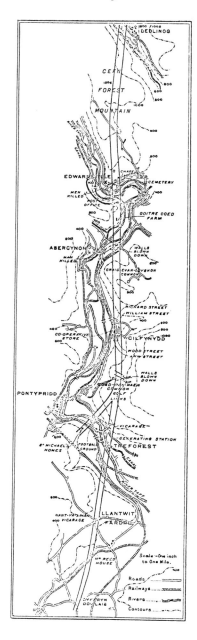

The course of the tornado which followed the Taff Valley in South Wales on 27 October 1913 for a distance of fifteen kilometres (H. Billett). The several small changes of path direction are reminiscent of those of the Dorset Cursus.

On the other hand, especially when travelling over undulating country, tornado tracks occasionally change direction more obviously, either abruptly or in a long sweeping bend, and sometimes this seems due to a change in the slope of the terrain.

Three other features of tornado tracks need mentioning. The first is a variation in breadth, where the track widens or narrows. This is found, too, in the cursuses at Springfield (Essex) and Fornham All Saints (Suffolk) among others, and is a well-known feature of the Stonehenge and the Dorset Cursuses. The second is a skipping effect in which a conspicuous obstruction, perhaps part of a farm or wood, escapes obvious damage due to a lifting of the foot of the twisting funnel above a part of the course. The tornado which I believe was responsible for the Drayton cursus in Oxfordshire may have skipped in this way, if the gap in its path dates from Neolithic times. A third characteristic is a tendency for the track to follow a long, gentle arc—which a team of surveyors would find vastly more difficult to engineer in the absence of the guiding curve of a tornado track than they would the already problematical feat of marking out a long straight line over hill and dale.

All the properties of tornado tracks described above have their parallels in the idiosyncrasies of the Neolithic cursuses, and the colossal Dorset Cursus includes most of them in the course of its great length.

6

The Path of the Sky God

Richard Atkinson has written, 'Of all the early prehistoric monuments of Britain the Dorset Cursus is both the largest and at the same time one of the least known.' In fact, not only is the mighty Dorset Cursus ill-known but, like the other cursuses of Britain, it is completely misunderstood. Only now, as the importance of the role of the spiralling tornado in the spiritual thought of the ancient Britons is being clarified, can the important role of the cursuses in the development of prehistoric British religion be assessed.

Unfortunately for Britain, nothing has come to us by way of traditions, sagas and literature from Neolithic and Bronze Age times, but clues exist in two stirring passages from the *Rig Veda*, the Sanskrit lore of praise which dates from the beginnings of Brahmanical India. Here we find that the all-powerful god of tornado, thunder and rain, Parjanya, is envisaged as a god of fertility, the origin of germination in plants, animals and women. As impregnator invincible he was likened to a bull. The first passage runs:

> The Bull, loud roaring, quick to send his gifts,
> sows in the plants the seed for
> germination.
> He smites the trees aside, he kills the demons:
> all things fear him who wields the

mighty weapon.
From him extremely strong run even the
righteous when thundering Parjanya
strikes the wicked.

Since he is, quixotically, the bearer of destruction and life-bearing seed, he is more than superficially similar to the cursus-making tornado god. He sounds like the ancient British Sky God, creator of the Dorset Cursus, the Stonehenge Cursus and those other cursus monuments of the Neolithic landscape.

Sing forth and praise Parjanya, Nirvana's son who
grants the gift of rain.
May he provide our grazing.
Parjanya is the one god who forms in cattle, mares,
in crops and soil and womanhood, the germ
of life.

Yet here the parallel diverges. In India Parjanya is a virile god of the male-dominant Indo-European Age, whereas the ancient British cursus god made his infrequent visits to earth in a Goddess-worshipping era. In Britain, Ireland and France the Great Goddess was the fountain and source of all life, and the Cursus God an occasional consort-impregnator, but when the union between God and Goddess took place it was climactic—that atmospheric moment when Sky blended with Earth. For the affected locality it was an exultant day in the lore of the Goddess—a day demanding to be memorialised by the anxious community —because first and foremost the cursus was a Goddess monument, built in honour of the day when she visibly received the Cursus God in holy union. In recognising the event as an act of Divine Marriage the cursus was celebrating the founding of the universe and the creation of life itself.

The Dorset Cursus merits detailed analysis because it can be demonstrated to what a considerable degree it influenced worship through the building of secondary monuments and because, perhaps surprisingly, it allows inferences to be drawn as to a possible date for the anniversary ceremonials. Stretching for 9.6 kilometres across Cranborne Chase in northern Dorset, it was built in the Earlier Neolithic period, about the middle of the fourth millennium. Much of Britain was then covered by dense woodland, broken only by islands of cultivation whose pattern shifted about as soils worsened and crop-yields fell, encouraging the farmers to attack fresh forest by, most likely, slash and burn methods.

Like all cursuses the Dorset Cursus is an elongated area enclosed by banks and external ditches. To complete the enclosure almost twenty kilometres of ditch were excavated by cutting through the thin turf to a depth of nearly two metres in the subsoil chalk. The best estimate of the labour required to dig the ditches and prepare the banks is that of D. W. A. Startin, who arrived at 450,000 man-hours. This mighty feat of engineering was followed by an extensive programme of barrow-building. In all, sixteen long barrows were constructed close to the cursus. Two of them are out of sight of it and may already have been there when it was built. Of the remaining fourteen, two are actually inside the cursus and all of them, apart from their ritual and ceremonial functions, must surely have been planned and positioned to serve as directional indicators. This point is indisputable because of their inbuilt compass orientations. Although time and the plough have not entirely spared them (four have been obliterated, and others may still lie hidden), their alignments can be found even when above-ground features are erased because the side-ditches scoured deep into the chalk are detectable by probing.

The cursus starts on Thickthorn Down in the parish of Gussage St Michael, ten kilometres north-east of the town of Blandford Forum. The causewayed camp of Hambledon Hill, twelve kilometres due west of the southernmost terminal of the cursus, is a major Neolithic site which was contemporary with the cursus, and the cursus builders would undoubtedly have made use of and assisted at whatever functions were arranged for Hambledon Hill.

The cursus terminal is marked by a triple-sided bank 80–100 metres in length, which is now 18 metres wide and two metres above the present bottom of the much-silted outer ditch. This is impressive for a bank that was never more than an unsupported heap of earth and chalk rubble and which has resisted the action of time and weather for 5,500 years. It is the best preserved section of the entire cursus. Close to the south-east are two long mounds of long-barrow type (called Gussage St Michael I and II) which seem to be an important part of the whole terminal construction scheme.

From windswept Thickthorn Down the cursus descends east-north-eastwards, in the guise of a former pair of low banks and ditches around a hundred metres apart. The ditches have long since disappeared, filled by the ceaseless action of weathering and farming, although at certain seasons their locations are visible from the ground or air by anomalies in vegetation growth. The cursus turns slightly with a south-easterly bias, and after a kilometre traverses watermeadows and a brook by Higher Farm. At this point, I should stress that neither a race-course nor a ceremonial way would from choice be directed into swampy meadows and across a stream, whereas any insensitive 'divine' tornado would carry on regardless.

The path of the cursus then bears straight up the slope of Gussage Hill to the conspicuous long barrow (Gussage St Michael III) built crossways within the

Aerial view of the terminal bank of the Dorset Cursus on Thickthorn Down. It is still in place after 5,500 years, but the cursus banks to its north have been obliterated. The long barrow on the right is Gussage St Michael I.

cursus on the hill crest. Because it is unique to find a long barrow inside a cursus, there must be a good reason for putting it there, and I believe that it played a vital role in the project.

After descending the far slope the cursus swerves slightly left, then right, and at the foot of the hill narrows before traversing a second broad valley, at which it bears left and crosses Wyke Down towards Bottlebush Down. At this point, on the slope just where the cursus changes direction more sharply to the left, and now 5.6 kilometres from Thickthorn, a cross-bank with an outer ditch once existed, in a style that may have resembled a terminus, but it had been destroyed and the ditch filled in antiquity, possibly by the people who built it. Oddly enough, the side ditches of the first or southern part of the cursus never met the side ditches of the northern part, leaving access causeways.

The cursus leaves this cross-bank with a slight change of direction and continues north-eastwards up and over the down. The original right-hand bank is visible here, following the field boundary and wire fence, as Richard Atkinson pointed out in 1955. Under this bank in Spring 1986, where a plough had recently

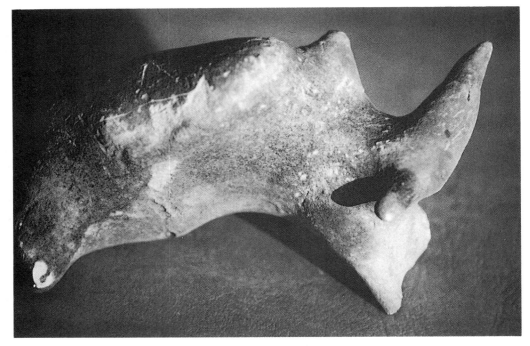

The natural piece of flint resembling a bull, found under the eastern bank of the Dorset Cursus which survives as a field boundary on Bottlebush Down.

cut into its side, I found a splendid naturally-shaped flint, sharply horned and resembling a charging, bellowing bull. It is possible that this flint had been selected and prized for its shape, and deposited or lost within the cursus bank thousands of years ago.

Beyond the down the cursus crosses fields, swinging left and then right into a third valley, after which it enters what is now a conifer plantation. Incorporated in the left-hand bank, with a small axial misalignment, is a fairly well-preserved long barrow, called Pentridge IV. It is 43 metres long. The orientation of the barrow differs from that of the cursus ditches by a clockwise rotation.

Richard Atkinson noticed that the principal irregularities occurred in the north-west ditch, and from this thought that the south-east side might have been 'ranged out and marked initially on the ground, the position of the other ditch being determined by offsets taken from the former at intervals, and evidently not always measured with equal accuracy'.

Although this argument seems logical, it does less than justice to the proven abilities of the Neolithic peoples in the art and practice of surveying. Communities that could align barrows with one another and with solar alignments could have made regular banks and ditches had they wished. The crucial point is that the obvious defects lie in the north-west ditch. Tornadoes spin anticlockwise and travel with the direction of the prevailing wind. This compounds the wind force on the right-hand side, and diminishes it on the left-hand side, creating a more perfect edge to the trail of tornado damage along the right, well known to tornado investigators, but an intermittently regular edge along the left. It is improbable that the builders progressed by offsetting; they followed as best they could the sides of the track left by the tornado. Richard Bradley suggests that Richard Atkinson may have over-generalised, for in the admittedly short section which he himself and others excavated on Wyke Down, the left-hand side was the more exact.

Continuing from the cursus barrow (Pentridge IV), the cursus runs fairly straight for a couple of kilometres, passing close to the village of Pentridge. Some 750 metres short of the terminal on Martin Down Richard Atkinson detected, by probing, gaps facing each other in the ditch-bank pairs. It is likely that, in order to avoid undignified clambering over bank and ditch, these causeways served as points of access for entry and exit. There is also the question of maintenance, of keeping the cursus free of trees and bushes for what may have amounted to hundreds of years, which could have been resolved by introducing grazing stock through the prepared gaps. This is perhaps the best explanation for the cursus gaps on both Martin Down and Bottlebush Down. Lastly, while still in Pentridge parish, the cursus swings slightly right and finishes on the level plain of Martin Down at a terminal earthwork which has now completely vanished.

This northern structure had squared banks. Aligned on its centre are as many as three nearby long barrows and a bank-barrow 152 metres long, suggesting that considerable importance was attached to this terminus, as to the southern end at Thickthorn. The fact that no barrows had been built near the cross-bank on Bottlebush Down would seem to indicate that it was considered insignificant. When the cursus is viewed as a whole, there is a surprising duplication of in-built alignments between the southern and northern parts, which would make sense if one imagined the work being carried out by co-operating tribal groups, one proceeding from the south and the other from the north, and that they met at Bottlebush!

Several writers have commented, without much enthusiasm, that cursuses may have been processional ways or funerary avenues, or that they may have served as enclosures or land divisions. A purely astronomical use was more energetically proposed by A. Penny and John Edwin Wood. Like previous workers, they assumed that the majority of long barrows were in place before the cursus was planned, and that it was cunningly woven between them, but the astronomical alignments are more likely to have come about by positioning the barrows after completing the cursus. There are also several non-astronomical alignments built into the scheme, which Penny and Wood missed because they limited their search to the more obvious solar and lunar alignments.

Richard Bradley thought that the cursus might have been built as part of an extended process of social change around 3500 BC, when restrictions on the privilege of monumental burial were increasing. He wondered if the building of the Dorset Cursus and nearby long barrows containing few or even no burials was an indication of the authority of the people who directed the operations. In the context of the prevailing Goddess religion, however, such corpseless mounds were probably built as ritually-consecrated shrines to serve as alignment indicators within the cursus-barrow complex; this would have been their primary function.

As I have noted, an estimate of 450,000 man-hours has been given for preparing the banks and ditches of the Dorset Cursus. This would have been more if the banks were vertically revetted with wood as Richard Bradley suggests, and even more if forest and scrub had to be cleared as well. Analysis of snails found in the ditch bottoms suggests a combination of grassland and open beechwood, supported by Richard Bradley who found that at points only 700 metres apart one length ran through mixed vegetation while another crossed a patch of closed woodland. A tornado would have created havoc with trees along its path and laid down a great number, but the clearance of broken, uprooted trees, besides scrub, would still have been a formidable task. Nonetheless, without the aid of tornado destruction the labour would have been far greater. It is significant that the southern terminal is known to have been built in open grassland.

Is it likely that the cursus project was undertaken so that the powerful could exert their authority over the workers? And with the aim of directing their attention to dummy mounds at the cursus terminals and nearby Wor Barrow, mounds which in earlier times had been intended as burial places and were being built empty or nearly empty to demonstrate the might of the community leaders? While all these non-tornado suggestions are inadequate, some of them do contain a degree of truth. The great cursus in Dorset is so preposterous in size, and so complex when examined, that outrageous explanations have been sought for it.

My theory is much simpler. The path of the Dorset Cursus, complicated though it is with its changes of direction and width, agrees with all that is known of tornado trails as they rise over hills, cross streams and rivers, and tear through copses and forests. Like all British cursuses the Dorset Cursus would have been built without prior planning. Work would have begun immediately following a tornado strike. God had come down to earth.

As a result, cursus building was intrinsically straightforward—no surveying, no advanced planning, simply the hard grind of digging. Chance directed the tornado path and its trail through the woods, scrubland and fields, and mankind followed the course where it went. Except in times of war there never was greater motivation in the history of human endeavour than that promoted by a religion, with its promise of life-after-death, as the supremely efficient way of exacting the maximum sweat and toil from mortals. Every cursus was made to be an everlasting memorial to a divine visit and at times may indeed have been used for commemorative ceremonies and processions. Astronomical alignments and tribal prestige also came into this.

An examination of the construction and purpose of the barrows in and around the Dorset Cursus throws an extraordinarily clear light on the underlying religious motivation. Although the monuments comprising the cursus complex are so numerous, few excavations have been made. A mere fourteen metres out of a total of 20,000 metres of the circumferential ditches of the cursus have been explored, and besides Wor Barrow, excavated by General Pitt-Rivers last century, the only excavated barrow is Gussage St Michael II on the crest of Thickthorn Down. Luckily, these excavations are very informative and, besides providing evidence of date, supply important evidence concerning fourth-millennium ritual and belief.

Gussage St Michael II (or Thickthorn barrow) was thoroughly excavated by C. D. Drew and Stuart Piggott in the late 1930s. The mound is aligned with the midwinter sunrise as seen from the forecourt of the nearby long barrow Gussage St Michael I, which is adjacent to the cursus's east terminal bank, and the alignment is perfect when account is taken of the positions of three pits if the latter were used as holes for stout posts for foresights as A. Penny and John Edwin Wood suggest. To watchers in the forecourt of the barrow adjoining the cursus the midwinter sun appeared to rise from the body of the second barrow at a distance of 300 metres. Such a sunrise could be regarded as a rebirth of the sun from the body of the Goddess. It is therefore remarkable that this barrow takes part in a second alignment as seen from the opposite direction. From Gussage St Michael VI, looking back to Gussage St Michael II, which again appears on the hillcrest, the sun is seen to set on midsummer's day—this time it sinks *into* the Goddess's body.

No interment was made in this barrow at the time of construction and, following Paul Ashbee, it is best described as an 'imitative ritual structure' or cult barrow. Its role in the religious scenario was to provide a mystical performance, and the deposits were plainly devotional. These included an exceptional chalk phallus with damaged glans, a second chalk object which is surely another phallus but with a glans so badly damaged that the lip alone survives, a skull with horn-cores of the urus or wild ox (*Bos primigenius*), two round neck-vertebrae of the wild ox, and various antler pieces and fragments, including 'a slice of

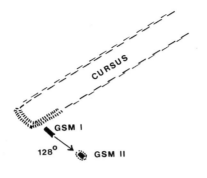

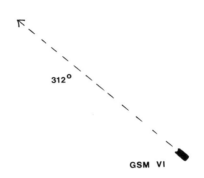

The south-western end of the Dorset Cursus known as the Thickthorn Terminal. The terminal is not at right angles to the banks of the cursus as one might expect, but is skewed round to 128 degrees from north, which is the direction of midwinter sunrise. The long barrows Gussage St Michael I and II also have this orientation. At the same time Gussage St Michael VI appears to be lined up with II, the direction of midsummer sunset.

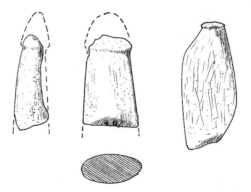

Chalk phalluses from the long barrow Gussage St Michael II now in Dorchester Museum (after Drew and Piggott). In both examples the glans has been worn away, or somehow broken off. Why?

antler cut and shaped by human agency'. Some of the bones were on the ditch bottom, and others beneath the mound scattered on the ancient turf with the carbonised remains of hawthorn branches and a log. As is usual with such deposits the horned skull is all that remains of a ritual offering of a complete bull's head. In this case it was probably intended for both the Goddess and the Cursus God.

The round vertebrae of the *Bos primigenius* had been selected for their size, and lay in black mould above the old turf line in the northern quadrant of the mound. The worshippers, who could not write, used symbols to accompany their prayers. Like the phalluses, the discs, which stood for testicles, were directed at masculine or Bull-God fertility. Vertebrae were also among the foundation deposits at Silbury Hill (c2660 BC) where they lay touching a big animal tooth. Similar findings are known for the early round barrow Winterslow 20 which is possibly of the early Beaker Period. In a shallow pit beneath the barrow, propped against a human skull, was a phallus of chipped flint, and inside the skull were two vertebrae, especially chosen and well positioned, which fell out when the skull was moved. Aubrey Burl suggested they were a fertility offering in view of 'the nearby flint mines'.

Few phalluses have been found from prehistoric Britain, so the Thickthorn examples are highly significant. However, I believe that the excavations of the future will produce many more. The only true Dorset Cursus long barrow to have been excavated (Thickthorn) produced two phalluses. Four of the Stonehenge Cursus long barrows were partially searched in the nineteenth century and produced one phallus of flint (Winterbourne Stoke I). One phallus of chalk is known from Alexander Keiller's Windmill Hill excavations near Avebury, and a possible bone phallus came from the Trundle, near Goodwood in Sussex. There are chalk phalluses from Durrington Walls near Stonehenge, from Grimes Graves flint-mines in Norfolk and a huge example from a ritual shaft at Maumbury Rings, Dorchester.

The Maumbury phallus lay with an antlered skull. The symbolism of this juxtaposition adds to the considerable evidence assembled by Marija Gimbutas and others that the antlered skull, like the bucranium, is a zoomorphic rendering of the shape of the uterus and thereby symbolic of the regenerative womb. Not far away, in South Dorset, there are phalluses from Mount Pleasant, and across the sea possibly an Irish one from Newgrange.

Balls of chalk or stone are even more common, and have been found at most of the sites just mentioned as well as at Stonehenge and a number of other monuments. Windmill Hill produced more than thirty, mostly in pairs, and among numerous others a bone ball, 30 mm in diameter, probably carved from a femur, and a sandstone ball, 38 mm in diameter, came from the Goddess

A phallus of chalk from Maumbury Rings Henge. *Photo courtesy of the Dorset Natural History and Archaeological Society, Dorset County Museum, Dorchester*

Chalk carvings of phalluses and balls from Mount Pleasant Henge.

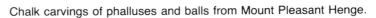

barrow on Anglesey called Bryn yr Hen Bobl. Carved balls were also found at Stoney Littleton long barrow in the nearby plough soil.

The Thickthorn phalluses, which can be seen in Dorchester County Museum, are unusual for the heavy damage suffered by the glans. It may be that they were used in some ceremony which involved striking or dragging them along the ground. Few of the other phalluses mentioned have suffered in this way (except the one from Mount Pleasant which is chipped at the tip of the glans). The damage to the Thickthorn objects may be linked with the origin of the cursus, particularly because the Thickthorn barrow was almost certainly a 'foundation barrow'. So besides the obvious fertility symbolism, there may have been a ritual imitating the behaviour of the Sky God's tornado-funnel when penetrating Earth. The phalluses could have been used to score the turf at the time of demarcating the limits of the new barrow. In prehistoric Assyria the phallic symbolism of a prayer was directed to the god 'whose plough has fertilised the earth'.

Therefore, just as the Hindus, among others, identified the furrow with the vulva and the seeds with semen, so there existed a widespread identification

A Bronze Age rock carving from Litsleby in Western Sweden. The ithyphallic ploughman and 'oxen' are depicted cutting three furrows in the fields of Goddess Earth, each furrow a symbolic vulva. This (three furrow) agricultural rite was widespread in Europe and persisted well into Christian times in many regions.

These Swedish rock carvings show the development of the idea, using images and symbols, that began with the cattle-drawn plough. Plough and spade being synonymous with penis, the wheeled farm implement is transformed into male genitalia, while the draught animals become the female opening. Simplicity reaches its logical limit in the picture below where the sexual organs are joined. So the action of ploughing proves to be equivalent to the consummation of marriage between Plough and Earth—as if between God and Goddess.

7. The phallus of the Storm God. A tornado funnel cloud over Hayling Island, Hampshire, on 27 October 1984. *Photo H.R. Lambie*

8. The Dorset Cursus, looking northwards across Bottlebush Down. The ploughed-out banks and ditches show up well, as does the Bottlebush crossbank. Along the centre-right a part of the original cursus bank survives.

9. The Greater Cursus, known as the Stonehenge Cursus, photographed from the air in 1987.

10. The sacred circles of Stonehenge seen from the air. The Heel Stone is at the top of the picture beside the main road.

11. The Midsummer Marriage. Three minutes after sunrise the shadow cast by the Heel Stone traverses the broad, central trilithon arch of the outer ring of stones, and penetrates the inner sanctum of the monument.

among agrarian communities of woman or the Goddess with the ploughed earth. Allusions to this belief survive to this day in European folklore. In the same way, the equation 'spade equals phallus' is so closely held that in some languages the roots of the words can only have been the same. There are many pictorial representations on the theme, like the Swedish rock-carving from Litsleby, which has the additional touch of a symbolic may-tree proffered by the man or god; the message of spring fertility extends even to the draught animals joined to the plough.

From the Danish Bronze Age there is a cremation urn-lid, found at Maltegard, which shows the meeting of man-and-woman or God-and-Goddess, again combined with the phallic may-tree, the whole symbolically framed within a life-bearing spiral or torque of leaves from the same tree of fertility. The lid of this urn is perforated with a round hole, evoking familiar female imagery.

The barrow known as Gussage St Michael III, 40 metres long, lies at right angles wholly within the cursus on the crest of Gussage Down. Although at this point the cursus banks and ditches have been ploughed away, probing shows that the width of the cursus here is about a hundred metres. The positioning of a transverse barrow with a 144° compass orientation so prominently on the hill-ridge was plainly intended to give it unrivalled visibility when viewed along the cursus both from the north-east and the south-west. The location and orientation of its companion barrow (Gussage St Michael IV) on the same 144° azimuth, 250 metres to the south-east, must also be significant.

A. Penny and J. E. Wood propose that the orientations of the cursus in this

Here the Sacred Wedding acquires a new twist—as rebirth symbolism on a Bronze Age cremation urn from Maltegaard, Denmark. The meaning of the message is heightened by the spiral character of the surrounding wreath, the presence of the may-tree, and the position of the hole in the middle.

region, whether measured from the south-west or north-east, are astronomically significant in that they correspond, respectively, to the least northerly moonrise (which is c60–61°) and least southerly moonset (238–239°) as viewed from the Thickthorn terminal towards Gussage or from Gussage towards Thickthorn. They imply that the orientation of the cursus was decided with such alignments in mind. This theory ignores the effect of atmospheric-refraction correction which makes risings earlier and settings later than they would otherwise be. The directions for midsummer sunrise and midwinter sunset are *not* exact opposites and neither are the lunar extremes, so these orientations of the cursus are more likely to be a chance result of the cursus trending from south-west to north-east. What is interesting is that by looking from the cross-bank, now erased, on Bottlebush Down the midwinter sun could be seen to set, as Penny and Wood correctly state, over the centre of the Gussage transverse barrow which stands proud on the skyline.

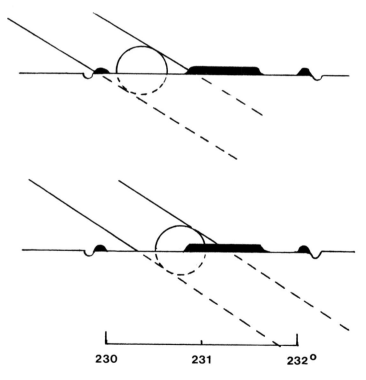

230   231   232°

Midwinter sunset over long barrow Gussage St Michael III in the Dorset Cursus. The viewing position was the centre of the Bottlebush cross-bank (upper diagram) and a point 20 metres north-west of the centre of the cross-bank (lower diagram).

Such a spectacle probably had a spiritual meaning. It could have been a stage-set in which landscape and sunset were manipulated in order that Sun and Earth, God and Goddess, might re-enact the mythology of the origin of the World. On midwinter's night the Goddess barrow on Gussage Down engulfed the sun, and 'detained' it for the sixteen hours of the long winter night before returning it to the waiting world the next day. This could be confirmed by priests, priestesses and other believers if they proceeded along the cursus to the platform of the Thickthorn terminal and the forecourt of Gussage St Michael I, in time to watch the midwinter sun rising 'from the Thickthorn barrow, Gussage St Michael II'. It may explain why the bank of the Thickthorn terminal is awkwardly skewed to match the midwinter sunrise direction because, although the cursus begins on a bearing 60° east of north, the terminal bank was *not* built at right angles to the cursus—that is, not at 60 + 90° = 150° as one would expect, but at 129±1°. Moreover, because Gussage St Michael I and II are both angled in

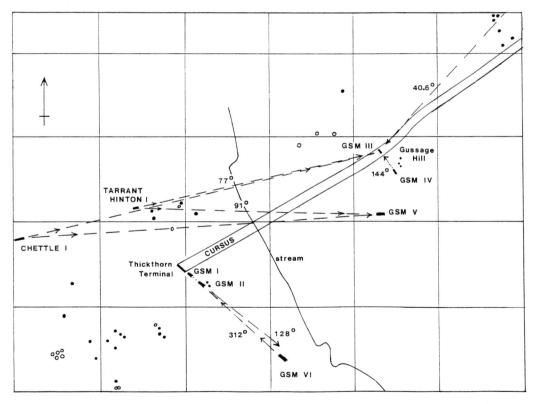

The Dorset Cursus. Plan of the south-western section showing the relationships between the long barrows and the cursus. Some of the round barrows are indicated as well.
© *Crown copyright*

the midwinter sunrise direction, their long shadows unite in a solar-terrestrial shadow spectacle.

Ritual reconstructions are highly speculative. We shall never know how far the underlying mythology had evolved, but a contrived manifestation like this would fit in with the beliefs and perceptions of an agrarian society, and it does account for all the known facts. As with Stone Age cultures from other communities and other continents, the ancient inhabitants of North Dorset would have devised a mythological base for their view of the birth of the world and of life. Re-enacting the myths holds the people to the divine; by reassuring the deities of the believers' goodwill, it placates them.

The relationships between the southern half of the cursus and its long barrows are significant. It can be no accident that all the barrows which are visible in conjunction with the cursus are orientated with it in some way. It follows that these barrows were built after the cursus was finished.

These orientations are summarised in Table II.

The key position occupied by these barrows is that of Tarrant Hinton I. Both it and Chettle I are aligned on Gussage St Michael III. Their common bearing is *almost* identical at 77° east of north. The event that was important was certainly sunrise over Gussage St Michael III as seen from both Chettle I and Tarrant Hinton I. It is remarkable and extremely important that because Tarrant Hinton I is 1.5 kilometres closer to Gussage Down than is Chettle I (three kilometres away compared with 4.5, their altitudes being similar), the sun rises slightly later for worshippers waiting at the former barrow. This explains why its azimuth is a little farther east of north, and confirms that the crucial point was to have the sun rise from behind Gussage St Michael III for people watching at both barrows. The slightly different azimuthal arrangement ensures that this happens *on the same day of the year* in both instances. This observation is crucial; its significance is clarified later in connection with another 77° orientation built into the northern part of the cursus.

To the east of Tarrant Hinton I, and at similar altitude, is Gussage St Michael V, itself aligned east-west and located as an equinoctial indicator on the false crest of a hillside four kilometres away (sadly it has been destroyed by the plough). The celebration dates here would have been the spring and autumn equinoxes. Tarrant Hinton I is 144° from Thickthorn terminal; this alignment parallels that of the mutual orientation between Gussage St Michael III and IV and their self-orientations, and it is also the self-orientation of the great bank barrow Pentridge II, discussed below. The meaning of 144° is another mystery to resolve.

The next barrow is Wimborne St Giles I, from which Gussage St Michael III can be seen on the west-south-western horizon. Although badly damaged, it was

TABLE II
Long barrows owing their orientations to the Dorset Cursus

BARROW NAME	GRID REF	LENGTH METRES	ORIENTATION	NOTES
Self-orientations and alignments of long barrows within view of Thickthorn Terminal or long barrow Gussage St Michael III (GSM III)				
Thickthorn Terminal	ST 96951243	c90	SE 130°	skewed to midwinter sun
Gussage St Michael I	ST 97031238	47	SE 131°	128° to GSM II (angled on midwinter sun)
Gussage St Michael II	ST 97181225	30	SE 127°	(a) 128° from GSM I (b) 320.5° to Tarrant I
Gussage St Michael III (barrow inside cursus)	ST 99301383	40	SE 144°	set transverse and 144° to GSM IV
Gussage St Michael IV (its companion)	ST 99471360	52	SE 144°	c144° from GSM III
Gussage St Michael V (obliterated)	ST 99271312	64	'E' n/d	91° from Tarrant I
Gussage St Michael VI (obliterated)	ST 98151140	26	'SSE' n/d	312° to GSM II (26° to GSM III)
Wimborne St Giles I (obliterated)	SU 015148	36	'E' n/d	(247° to GSM III)
Chettle I	ST 95051280	98	ENE 77°	77° to GSM III
Tarrant Hinton I (obliterated)	ST 96451318	c30	ENE n/d	77° to GSM III 91° to GSM V 140.5° to GSM II (c144° to terminal)
The cross-bank on Bottlebush Down				
Bottlebush Bank	SU 01571566	c90	SE c129°	(midwinter sunrise) c231° to GSM III (midwinter sunset)
Self-orientations and alignments of barrows within view of Pentridge Terminal				
Pentridge Terminal	SU 04021921	c90	SE c129°	(midwinter sunrise) 144° to P II 163° to P I
Pentridge IV (within cursus bank)	SU 02571695	43	NE c49°	midsummer sunrise −77° to Wor Barrow also 40/40.5° to P I
Pentridge I (south of terminal)	SU 04151876	102	SSE 163°	P I + P III cross at terminal

TABLE II – CONTINUED

BARROW NAME	GRID REF	LENGTH METRES	ORIENTATION	NOTES
Pentridge II (the bank barrow)	SU 04101910	152	SE 144°	144° points to terminal
Pentridge III (north of terminal)	SU 03941951	29	SSE c163°	P I + P III at 163° cross at terminal 231° sunset over Wor Barrow
Handley I (Wor Barrow)	SU 01241728	46	SE c148° 231°	−77° from P IV midsummer sunset from P III
Martin I	SU 035204	53	SSE 159°	159° points to terminal
Broadchalke II (in Wiltshire)	SU 03412114	23	'E' n/d	163° to terminal 163° to P I + P III

Round barrow that may have been added very late to introduce further alignments

Gussage All Saints 12 (Berends Barrow)	SU 01381626			40.6° from GSM III (most southerly moonrise) 218.2° from P III (most northerly moonset)

Long barrows out of view of the cursus but possibly related to it

Child Okeford I	ST 845127	73	SSE 163°	in causewayed enclosure on Hambledon Hill
Child Okeford II	ST 849120	26	SE n/d	

NOTES

1 n/d means not determined. GSM V, GSM VI, Tarrant Hinton I and Wimborne St Giles I are all levelled; ditch probing is needed in order to recover their self-orientations.

2 For Tarrant Hinton I Leslie V. Grinsell (in *Dorset Barrows*) states that the side ditches seen on air photographs give (about) ENE (which could mean 77°); O/S maps give 141°.

3 *Possible anniversary date indicator:* The sunrise over GSM V at 77° as viewed from Tarrant Hinton I (about 20 August, or 20 April); and sunset over Wor Barrow (−77°) as viewed from Pentridge IV.

4 *Possible anniversary time-of-day indicator:* The altitude of the sun in the direction of Pentridge I (163°, c11 a.m.) as viewed from Pentridge terminal, or Pentridge III, and probably Broadchalke II; 163° is also the self-orientation of Pentridge I.

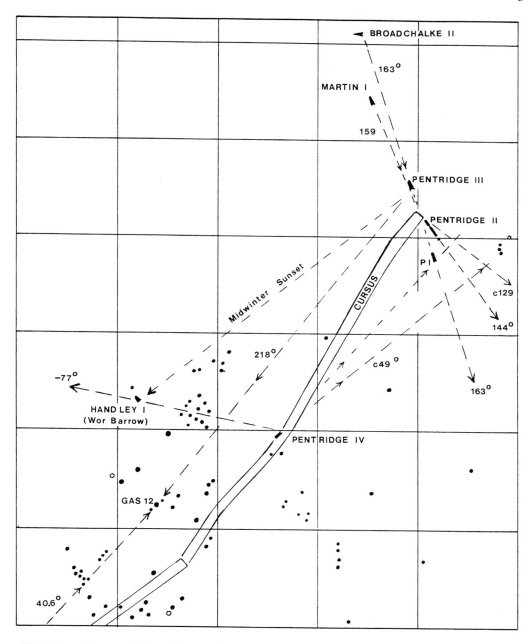

The Dorset Cursus. Plan of the north-eastern section giving the relationships between the long barrows and the cursus. The positions of some round barrows are indicated, including Gussage All Saints 12 (GAS 12). © *Crown copyright*

still a metre high when described in 1959 by Leslie Grinsell in his *Dorset Barrows*, where he added that the south-west was ploughed out. But when I visited it in 1986 I found it had been obliterated. Its orientation appears to have been WSW-ESE, so it too was probably aligned on Gussage III whose bearing is 247° from north, equalling west-south-west.

As for Gussage St Michael VI, from which Gussage St Michael III can be seen, it has been almost effaced from the landscape by modern farming. Leslie Grinsell gives SSE-NNW but to me it looks nearer to SE-NW. Because of growing crops I was unable to verify the self-orientation of Gussage St Michael VI by probing for the ditches, but was able to photograph instead the dismal spectacle of a tractor passing over it and destroying it further. It could be significant that 312°, which is the direction of Gussage St Michael II as seen from Gussage St Michael VI, is close to the direction of midsummer sunset. In other words, in the same way that the midwinter sun rises over Gussage St Michael II when viewed from Gussage St Michael I, so the midsummer sun sets over Gussage St Michael II when viewed from Gussage St Michael VI.

At the northern terminal of the Dorset Cursus five long barrows are aligned on the mid-point of the terminal cross-bank. The enormous barrow Pentridge II, originally 152 metres in length (but now cleft in two) and known as a bank barrow because of its length, is the most obvious one, and it is notable that its orientation of about 144° is the third time that this is found built into the cursus-barrow system. Once again a bank barrow signifies a direction which must have been crucially important to the designers. It happens that this is the direction of moonrise when the moon comes over the substantial elevation of Pentridge Hill at the moon's most southerly point in the Metonic cycle, an orientation that is not unexpected in view of the solidarity of the agrarian concept of goddess/earth/moon with fruitfulness and fertility, which thereby requires the moon in the choreography.

The axes of Pentridge I and Pentridge III and the position of the equinoctial barrow Broadchalke II (which is two kilometres away in South Wiltshire) are all aligned on the middle of the cursus terminal with a common azimuth of 163°. There must have been a motivation for this repeated patterning, but as this orientation lies beyond the extreme limits attainable for sunrise or moonrise one must seek a solution elsewhere. The prime candidate is that it could somehow serve as an 'anniversary indicator'.

A reasonable conjecture is that the 163° alignment was chosen to mark the time of day at which the cursus-creating tornado occurred, so that on the anniversary day of the tornado descent, when festive celebrations were under way to commemorate the Consummation of Marriage by the Sky God, the priests, priestesses and cursus builders were able to specify the time as well as the date

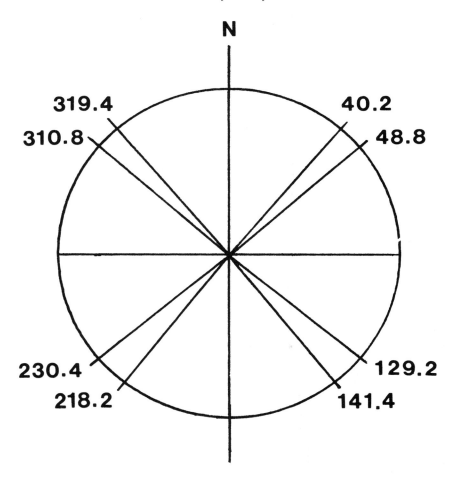

The extreme solar and lunar rising and setting positions for the latitude of the Dorset Cursus in 3500 BC (the various angles are measured clockwise from north). The calculations were done for half-orb elevations and a level horizon, but in the presence of hills the orb rises later and sets earlier than indicated by these angles.

of the anniversary. If so, then 11 o'clock in the morning is the critical moment because this is the hour when the sun's direction attains a bearing of 163° east of north.

It could be significant that 163° is also the self-orientation of the 73-metre bank barrow on Hambledon Hill, the Neolithic causewayed enclosure far out of sight to the west of the cursus. Could this additional provision for a 163° pointer have turned the bank barrow into an indicator for an assembly on Hambledon Hill of those who were unable to go to the cursus at the time of day when the worshippers at the cursus were celebrating their Sky God festival?

If so, what then might have been the day of the year? How could the cursus planners have exactly specified the anniversary day?

In speculating on the likely anniversary date I have started with the supposition that on that momentous day of the spiralling tornado the spectators marched along the tree-strewn tornado-path wondering how best to register the date of the event for posterity. They probably agreed on marking a place from which they could observe the sun setting over some conspicuous feature on the horizon. In its final form Wor Barrow (known also as Handley I) post-dates the cursus, perhaps by more than a century, but Wor Barrow was built on the site of a more ancient mortuary house which is likely to be distinctly older than the cursus. Moreover, Wor Barrow is on the western skyline for observers who follow the course of the tornado-cursus southwards from Pentridge.

The key to the solution may lie in the long barrow named Pentridge IV, which is bizarrely situated in the cursus wall and uncharacteristically breaks the monotony of the northern bank-and-ditch at this point. When standing in the forecourt of this barrow, if the sun is in the west-north-west it can be seen to set over Wor Barrow for an azimuth of 283°. Astoundingly, this is equivalent to 77° measured anticlockwise from due north—the same as the 77° sunrise alignment planned into the southern end of the cursus where 77° is the direction of that other barrow built inside the cursus, Gussage St Michael III, as seen from Chettle I and Tarrant Hinton I. I therefore propose that the anniversary sunset position was fixed for eternity by building Pentridge IV into the side of the cursus, its position facilitating the ceremonial for the most significant event on the cursus calendar.

It is true of course that the 77° sunset-sunrise azimuth happens twice annually —firstly around 20 April and later around 20 August. Which date is the more probable on tornado theory? By considering the frequency of severe tornadoes in relation to date (taken from the records of the Tornado and Storm Research Organisation), the probability is overwhelming that the tornado occurred in mid- to late August rather than mid- to late April.

We now know enough to attempt a reconstruction of the building sequence of the key barrows at the northern end of the cursus. Firstly, the position of Pentridge IV, the barrow in the cursus bank, was decided in relation to the mortuary house (77°) which would later be replaced by Wor Barrow, at which time its self-orientation was chosen to be midsummer sunrise which was 49° in prehistoric times.

The 129–130° skew taken by the Pentridge terminal bank was made to conform with the direction of midwinter sunrise. Pentridge III, with its 163° alignment, may have come next to serve as a time-of-day memorial. Its distance to the north of the Pentridge terminal was dictated by the need to observe the midwinter sunset over the same mortuary house. For 3500 BC the calculated direction of this sunset (which is 230.8°) is precisely right for the point where the sun reaches the horizon and is still close (at 231.1°) for the half-disc position.

The distance of Pentridge I from the terminal was decided later so that, as viewed from Pentridge IV, the moon would rise over it when at its most northerly point of the 18-year moon cycle (40–40.5°). The great bank barrow Pentridge II came later and preserved the alignment required by the moonrise for its most southerly rising. Martin I, which also points to the Pentridge terminal, and equinoctial Broadchalke II (whose azimuth to the terminal is 163°) could have been introduced at any time later.

There is just one other alignment to consider—that towards a 'conical' barrow, called Berends Barrow or Gussage All Saints 12, as seen from Gussage St Michael III. This barrow, as noted by A. Penny and J. E. Wood, appears to be an early bowl barrow. It could have been added decades or centuries afterwards in order to preserve the direction of extreme northerly moonrise as seen from Gussage St Michael III (calculated to have an azimuth of 40.5° as against the 40.6° measured) and the extreme southerly moonset as seen from Pentridge III (218.5° compared with 218.2° measured).

Although the myths which determined the building and operation of the Dorset Cursus will never be known, a logical sequence of development is nonetheless apparent:

1. A tornado strike to the locality was interpreted as Divine Revelation and construed as the Cosmic Consummation of the Gods. The cursus was laid out as a pair of parallel banks and ditches to mark the path of the spiralling winds, a track intended to last for eternity. By viewing it as the place of consummation between Sky God and Goddess, the cursus could equally be recognised as the vulva of the Great Goddess herself.

2. As the cursus was being built, a search for further meaning was made. At Thickthorn a platform terminal some 80–100 metres long was constructed and angled toward midwinter sunrise. Gussage St Michael I was built close by and from it the direction of midwinter sunrise was precisely obtained by setting up stout posts on a ridge south-east of the terminal on Thickthorn Down. When the posts had served their purpose a ritual barrow (Gussage St Michael II) was raised above the place where the posts had stood. Ten kilometres away, at the northern end of the cursus, the midwinter sunrise alignment was duplicated by the angle of the Pentridge terminal bank (angle c129°, length about 100 metres).

3.   On Gussage Down, within the cursus, Gussage St Michael III was raised transversely on the highest part of the ridge to be visible from all directions. At a point 250 metres away, an externally-sited barrow, orientated on the same azimuth (Gussage St Michael IV), linked the cursus-barrow to the world beyond. This could signify the intention to introduce the moon, the direction being that of the extreme southerly position at which the moon can ever rise.

4.   In the region where Bottlebush Down meets Wyke Down a cross-bank or pseudo-terminal was built. It is not known at what period in antiquity it was destroyed but it certainly did not have the importance of the Thickthorn and Pentridge terminals because no bank barrows or long barrows were ever built to serve it. It could have acted as an observation platform from which to watch midwinter sunset over the Gussage transverse barrow. At this point breaks in the cursus ditches were left in order to permit access to the interior of the cursus. It is possible that the 80–100 metre long cross-bank was angled on the midwinter sunrise (orientation c128–130°). The position of this observation post was not too critical. Any point within a kilometre to the south would have worked as well, but the place selected was where the cursus kinked and it was about the farthest north allowable. The small role played by this cross-bank shows that Bottlebush was never intended as a termination to the southern part of the cursus; the whole cursus, south and north, was built in one go and the barrows planned accordingly.

5.   It was arranged that the barrow Pentridge IV, in the cursus wall, should have an axial misalignment relative to the cursus so that it could face midsummer sunrise (49°) and be used for midsummer ceremonials. From its forecourt the sun was seen to set over Wor Barrow when the azimuth is 283° or −77°; this could be an anniversary date indicator for the mid- to late August sunset (or mid- to late April sunset). When the long barrow at Tarrant Hinton was built it was planned to view the sunrise over Gussage St Michael III for the sunrise azimuth of 77°. Chettle I duplicated this arrangement. The importance accorded to Tarrant Hinton barrow was expressed by arranging for it to align at 144° with the Thickthorn terminal, and by siting Gussage St Michael V to the east as a marker for the equinoxes.

6.   The cursus was terminated at Pentridge on Martin Down by a true terminal bank, angled at about 129° (midwinter sunrise alignment). Three long barrows were built nearby in conjunction with it during the ensuing years. Each barrow was directed to point at the centre of the terminal bank. The 152-metre long bank barrow was aligned on 144°, roughly the direction of the extreme southerly moonrise for this location relative to the height of Pentridge Hill. The other pair

lie on a mysterious 163° direction, which may have served as a time-of-day indicator but is otherwise inexplicable.

All the barrows display either calendrical or major solar or lunar properties. Probably few or none of the long barrows or bank barrows associated closely with the Dorset Cursus were intended to house any dead. They were to varying degrees best regarded as shrines or ritual monuments to the Goddess.

7

The Gate of the Gods

Most cursuses cannot be seen under ordinary circumstances. Their simple banks were ploughed away during four thousand years of farming activity, which explains why many cursuses were only found following the start of serious aerial archaeology some seventy years ago. In the few places where cursus banks survive, it is usually because of their later use as field boundaries.

The positions of British cursuses relative to Neolithic monuments, particularly large causewayed camps and long barrows, are a sign that they date from the same period. We also know that some cursuses had served their purpose and become obsolete by the Early Bronze Age, because their ditches had filled and the reduced banks were overlain by Bronze Age henges, rings, and work areas. Unfortunately so few cursuses have been excavated that fairly precise dating is rarely possible, but the limited excavations carried out on cursuses at Maxey (Cambridgeshire), Springfield (Essex), Dorchester-on-Thames (Oxfordshire), Stonehenge (Wiltshire), Thornborough (Yorkshire) and a few others (Drayton, Llandegai, Rudston, Lechlade, Findern) besides the Dorset Cursus, at least provide a guide to absolute ages. The indications are that cursus construction and use were largely confined to that part of the Earlier and Later Neolithic era covered by the second half of the fourth and much of the third millennium BC, and that cursuses probably began to be abandoned in some areas centuries earlier than in others.

Two early cursuses were those at Maxey and Thornborough. Despite its uniform appearance, the Thornborough cursus yields a vital clue in favour of a 'Sky-God' origin, while the excavations at Maxey have thrown up further evidence of an early bull-cult.

The Maxey cursus in Cambridgeshire may be the oldest identified so far—the middle of the fourth millennium BC or possibly earlier. Its width is 58 metres, but because of partial destruction by modern gravel working its full length is unknown, although it was not less than 1.8 kilometres. Contemporary with the cursus were two rings of ritual pits, one inside and one outside the cursus, and a sherd of Mildenhall pottery of mid-Neolithic date was found in a pit of the cursus pit-ring. When this ring of ten pits was being prepared, one of the pits cut into the cursus ditch and some of its spoil fell into the ditch in which there was only a little silt at the time, proving that it could not have been there long.

Two hundred metres south were two early henges where mid-Neolithic Mildenhall pottery has been found (presumed to be contemporary with and not much later than the cursus). A complete, horned ox-skull had been buried in a henge ditch as part of a consecration rite, implying a developed form of bull-worship, and there were also two polished antler horns and a deer rib, each carved with zigzags or chevrons in the manner of the portal stones at the Irish passage-graves of Newgrange, Knowth and Fourknocks, and of various cist slabs from the Orkneys. Like spirals and lozenges, zigzags and chevrons were universal symbols, linked to Goddess belief, which were common to Neolithic culture everywhere, bearing symbolic meanings of abundance and strength. The Boyne Valley and Orkney structures also date from the mid-fourth millennium.

The Yorkshire cursus at Thornborough is equally important, for this one followed a curving path through a forest. It lies on the western edge of the Vale of York, eight kilometres north-west of Ripon, and is exceptional among cursuses in having the banks thrown up outside the ditches. Three grand henges and numerous barrows nearby bear witness to a substantial community and spiritual life in the region. When one of these Bronze Age henges, the middle one, was constructed, it covered part of the cursus which must therefore have been ancient and out of use by that time.

The cursus runs from west-south-west to east-north-east for not less than 800 metres, with a width of 65 metres, the ditches regular and steadily curving. If it seems incredible that a primitive society should have been able to carry out accurate *linear* surveying up hill and down dale, how much more amazing that they should have created a smooth and regular curve several hundred metres long! Would it not be thought nigh impossible in view of the fact that the cursus was cut through a forest?

No such problems of credibility arise if one accepts that cursus paths derive

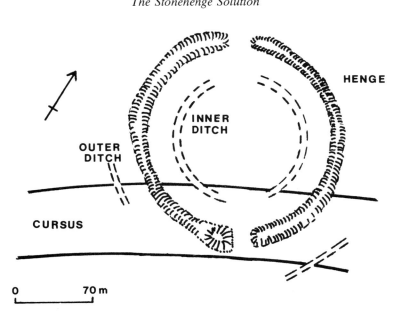

HENGE

INNER
DITCH

OUTER
DITCH

CURSUS

0   70 m

Thornborough Henge and the part of the 70-metre wide cursus which it overlies.
Excavation has shown that the henge was cut centuries after the cursus. Note
the curving ditches of the cursus.

from tornado tracks. Wherever the tornado went, whatever forest it cut through,
the local population had but to follow the path, and dig the trenches as they
went. And in the case of the Thornborough cursus, we know that it curved
through deciduous forest thanks to I. W. Cornwall's analysis of the Neolithic
fillings of the pre-henge cursus deposits. He concluded that the cursus ditches
were cut into the subsoil gravel, and that the copious humus in the lowest fillings
indicated deciduous forest with an abundance of drifted leaves. The ditches had
evidently become filled and grass-covered a considerable time before the bank
of the central circle was laid over them. In short, the cursus cut through woodland
(just as a tree-felling tornado would do), and the time interval between cursus
and henge was so great, of the order of a thousand years, that the cursus was
no longer in use when the henge superseded it. The beliefs of the Neolithic
cursus builders had either advanced or been overwhelmed by those of the Bronze
Age henge and round barrow makers. Farther south, at Maxey, the early cursus
was also out of use by the time that a Bronze Age mound was laid over it.

A peculiarity of at least the central henge at Thornborough was that the banks
had been liberally sprinkled with gypsum so as to whiten them. There was
no chalk there. As it was limestone country, the excavator, Nicholas Thomas,
suggested that the whitening was done in imitation of the henge banks of the

chalk downland, as in Wessex. If this is true, then the achievements of the men of Dorset and Wiltshire had spread far and wide. Thomas points to the discovery of a distinctive riveted-handle knife of Wessex type, found in four Yorkshire barrows, as a plain statement of close cultural contacts between Wessex and Yorkshire.

D. P. Dymond made another significant point: that the Neolithic and Bronze Age populations of central and west Yorkshire were not very high to judge from the distribution of finds and barrows compared with other regions. 'This includes the Ripon area despite its concentration of ritual monuments, and suggests that the siting of some ritual monuments at least was determined by predominantly religious considerations, and not by the presence of sizeable populations.' Again, this is what one would expect on a cursus-tornado theory. The tornadic whirlwind strikes at random. If the nearest communities wished to make a sanctuary following a tornado strike, they would have no choice but to take the few opportunities as they arose, regardless of distance or convenience.

How, then, does the cursus-tornado theory stand up to scrutiny? The majority of cursuses are shorter than two kilometres. Many are straight or composed of straight sections, sometimes with small deviations of direction or width. The 800 metres of the Thornborough cursus curve gently for the whole of its length. There is nothing in any of the cursuses which debars the possibility of their having been constructed by pursuing a tornado trail across the landscape. The small directional change that sometimes happens in the lee of a hill is familiar to tornado investigators, but as a property of the long Dorset Cursus this oddity has been a puzzle for cursus theorists.

Tornadoes which rip through a forest tear down the trees as they go. This very act, at once typical of the lofty whirlwind and Cursus God and which so terribly ravishes the Earth, immensely lightens the toil of forest clearance. The problem, sometimes voiced, concerning the need for the laborious removal of trees in the largely-forested Early Neolithic landscape, believed to be essential before cursus building could begin, evaporates before the destructive whirlwind which cuts its corridor through the mixed vegetation and trees. Moreover, the tornado is oblivious of swamp and river. So, it would appear, is the cursus.

As we have seen, the Dorset Cursus traverses the marsh of Gussage St Michael and its chalk stream. The Stanwell/Heathrow cursus, 3.5 kilometres long and 20 metres wide, if it is not a mistaken Roman road as has been suggested (although its southern rounded terminal and the finding of Late Neolithic Mortlake pottery in the ditch-fill argue against that), crosses two rivers, the Colne and the Wraysbury, west of Heathrow Airport. These rivers are deep and wide with a flood plain between, and there must have been a considerable amount of water in this part of the cursus four thousand years ago.

The Drayton cursus in Oxfordshire seems to be in two parts, formed by a tornado which lifted from the ground, crossed a stream and struck along the same line of attack a couple of hundred metres farther on. In Yorkshire one of the Rudston cursuses crosses a major chalk stream, the Gypsey Race.

The Rudston complex of prehistoric monuments, with its innumerable funeral, ritual and domestic sites and Britain's tallest standing stone eight metres high, is notable for four apparent cursuses within a 100 square-kilometre area. Their dimensions and orientations are quite different, and three of them cross watercourses. This suggests that during the long period of belief in the Cursus Sky God four tornadoes struck the region and were memorialised by cursus construction. A small part of one of them, Rudston A, was excavated by D. P. Dymond. Sinuous at the start, its 70-metre wide track aims northwards before tracking north-north-east across the Gypsey Race, a stream which is also crossed by Cursus C coming from the west.

Sherds from the bottom of the western ditch of Cursus A were of Beaker ware, with its characteristic twisted cord impressions and comb-marked lozenge patterns. This proves that the third millennium Beaker people made use of the cursus, if they did not also build it. No Neolithic pottery was found in the ditch-fill where it was excavated, but there was plenty in the banks and in the field. It is possible that the cursus was built by the Beaker people in the Early Bronze Age, but they may merely have been re-cutting or cleaning an earlier monument, especially when this cursus is compared with the timing of events at Thornborough. Because the other Rudston cursuses have not been excavated their age can only be guessed at, but the region is known to have had a fairly high population in the Neolithic Age. At any rate Rudston A could be one of Britain's latest cursuses dated so far, and if its use by the Beaker folk indicates a continuity of belief in the Neolithic Sky God into Bronze Age times, this must be highly significant for regional religious studies.

In view of the importance attached to the religious meaning of cursuses—notably, their role in the mystical concept of the Marriage of the Gods—it would be natural for every community to want its own cursus as proof that it, too, had been favoured by a visitation from the Sky God, and that the Cosmic Union between God and Goddess had taken place on its territory. I therefore started looking at parts of central southern England where cursuses seem to be lacking despite having been densely inhabited in Neolithic and Bronze Age times. The areas which chiefly interested me were the Windmill Hill/Avebury region of North Wiltshire, and the region of South Dorset in the neighbourhood of Dorchester and Maiden Castle.

We know that the Dorchester area is extremely rich in all classes of monument from the Neolithic and Bronze Ages. Only a cursus is missing, and yet long barrows and bank barrows are present in much the same way as those which accompany the great cursus between Thickthorn and Pentridge in North Dorset.

Several kilometres west of Dorchester, in the parish districts of Long Bredy and Kingston Russell, four important Neolithic barrows are grouped together, three of which are barrows of the greatly elongated type called bank barrows. The longest of the group, Long Bredy I, has a length of 198 metres. The Kingston Russell bank barrows, each about 80–90 metres long, are a kilometre to the south-east. In addition there is a distant bank barrow, Broadmayne I, 185 metres long, which is thirteen kilometres from the Kingston Russell barrows. The remains of another bank barrow, the longest of all at 550 metres, lie within the Neolithic causewayed enclosure and Iron Age hillfort of Maiden Castle, nine kilometres east of Kingston Russell. This barrow traverses the banks of the causewayed enclosure and is the only bank barrow to have been excavated using modern methods—by Mortimer Wheeler in the late 1930s. Because of my discovery that a large number of long barrows and bank barrows point to the terminals of their respective cursuses, I wondered whether a similar situation might prevail west of Maiden Castle in the neighbourhood of the Long Bredy and Kingston Russell bank-barrow groups.

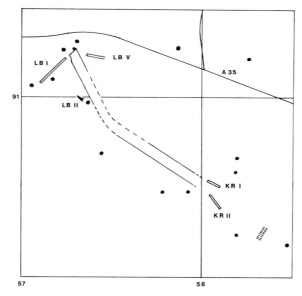

The course of a possible cursus in the south of Dorset and its relationship with two bank barrows in Kingston Russell County Parish and two bank barrows (one erased) in Long Bredy County Parish. The site of the south-eastern cursus terminal (if there was one) is unclear, but a clue survives in the combined orientations of long barrow Long Bredy I and the Kingston Russell bank barrows. © *Crown copyright*

Looking north-west from the Kingston Russell barrows towards the 200-metre Long Bredy I bank barrow on the skyline. The low-angle illumination of the winter wheat in the late-afternoon sunshine reveals what may be the vestiges of a pair of ploughed-out cursus banks.

I did my main fieldwork in the autumns and winters of 1985–86 and 1986–87, when the winter cereal crops in the fields north-west of the Kingston Russell bank barrows had grown sufficiently (to a height of 40 to 80 millimetres) for their growth pattern to accentuate the effects of the residual ancient banks and ditches of a cursus if it existed.

To my excitement, changes in crop growth revealed the presence of a pair of banks and external ditches, 43–45 metres apart, crossing the fields north-west of the Kingston Russell bank barrows as if coming from the Long Bredy barrows. In the light of the low late-afternoon sunshine, along a length of 200 metres, the inner bank on the northern side casts a distinct shadow of its own. The distant long barrow Long Bredy II was almost exactly aligned with this half of what seemed to be a cursus. I did not locate the ploughed-out terminal ditch of the cursus, but it may have been just west of the present field boundary, with remains of the terminal bank east of this boundary, possibly angled. If this is where it is, and it can hardly be any farther east without intruding on the physical presence of the Kingston Russell bank barrows, then both bank barrows point directly at this terminal. When looking south-east from Long Bredy I a kilometre to the north-west, these same features can be seen in the distance.

The region of the northern terminal of the cursus, in the vicinity of Long Bredy I, is now under pasture. Here help has come from air photographs taken many years ago when the land was arable and long before that when it was under grass. In 1971 a photograph by Roger Peers was published which revealed vestiges of ditch features at Long Bredy showing up as cropmarks. One set of marks delineated a long narrow region, about 130 metres by 21 metres, which came to be tentatively ascribed to a cursus (by C. J. Bailey and by Richard Bradley). However, these dimensions are not typical of cursuses and it is my opinion that they correspond very well with what would be expected of a ploughed-out bank barrow—a companion barrow to Long Bredy I. Therefore, in accordance with standard nomenclature I shall refer to it as Long Bredy V.

With this new understanding the origins of other field markings in the vicinity become clearer. The remains of the cursus terminal and 200 metres of ditches can be seen on an aerial photograph by J. K. St Joseph, published in 1959 by Leslie Grinsell in *Dorset Barrows*. The cursus terminal is fifty metres long and its direction skewed to agree with the alignment of bank barrow Long Bredy I. The apparent cursus runs south-eastwards and changes direction quite abruptly after passing a simple long barrow, Long Bredy II. The total length of the cursus is 1,050 metres. With the ploughed-out feature which I call Long Bredy V reinterpreted as a bank barrow, its role in the planning can be understood, because it points to the cursus terminal like its neighbour does, and just as the long barrows at Pentridge in North Dorset do. This possible new cursus therefore appears to be accompanied by four bank barrows, two at each end, all pointing directly at the terminals. I have provisionally named this monument the South Dorset Cursus.

The self-alignments of the various barrows tally with what I found at the Dorset Cursus. The sacred, northern terminal of the cursus is skewed approximately to the most northerly rising of the moon for 3500 BC, but it must be admitted that this could be a coincidence (its orientation seems to be 44° instead of 40°, but the error could have arisen because the measurement could only be made at 18-year intervals). The great length of Long Bredy I reinforces the same alignment. Its prominent hill-ridge location may have served to facilitate the discernment of the smaller 'sacred terminal' for people observing over great distances. Part way along the cursus is the long barrow Long Bredy II with an orientation close to that of midwinter sunrise, while at the southern end of the cursus Kingston Russell II has roughly the compass direction of the most southerly moonrise. This leaves Kingston Russell I (114°) and the obliterated Long Bredy V (c100–110° not yet accurately measured). The direction of one of these barrows (or both if the bearings turn out to be the same) may be a sunrise or sunset anniversary indicator. Farther afield are four other long barrows which appear to come within the orbit of the same people who built the possible cursus (Table III). One of these, Long Bredy IV (known locally as the Grey Mare and her Colts), is a damaged long barrow with chamber and likely crescent-shaped forecourt at its south-eastern end. It is a typical Goddess barrow, aligned on the midwinter sunrise, at which Sacred Marriage rites doubtless took place.

TABLE III
Details of barrows near the possible South Dorset Cursus

Barrow Name	Grid Ref	Length metres	Self-orientation by compass	Bearing to Cursus
Long Bredy I	SY 57189116	198	NE 44°	44° to NW terminal
Long Bredy V	SY 57409122	c130	ESE c102–110°	c102–110° to NW term
Long Bredy II	SY 57329099	34	ESE 126°	122° to SE terminal
Kingston Russell I	SY 58069052	92	ESE 114°	114° to SE terminal
Kingston Russell II	SY 58079042	77	SE 140°	140° to SE terminal
DISTANT BANK BARROWS				
WSM I (Maiden Castle)	SY 66858850	550	E c103°?	103° to SE terminal
Broadmayne I	SY 70288533	185	ESE 112°	113° to SE terminal
DISTANT LONG BARROWS				
W/borne Steepleton I	SY 60448836	55	SE n/d	132° to NW terminal
W/borne Steepleton II	SY 61418970	45	cE? n/d	109° to NW terminal
Winterborne Abbas I	SY 60459006	45	cE? n/d	102° to SE terminal
				111° to NW terminal
Long Bredy IV (Grey Mare and her Colts)	SY 58398706	25	SE n/d	164° to NW terminal
				174° to SE terminal
CURSUS TERMINALS				
NW terminal	SY 57289024	c50	NE 44°	
SE terminal	SY 580905	c45	not known	

NOTES

1   The self-orientations of WSM I (Winterborne St Martin I, at Maiden Castle) and Long Bredy V are imperfectly known at the time of writing; the bearings given are estimates from maps and photographs.

2   n/d means not determined.

One may ask whether the distant bank barrows at Broadmayne and Maiden Castle could have formed part of the same tornado-cursus scenario. Although the great bank barrow Broadmayne I is thirteen kilometres from the South Dorset Cursus, strangely enough its self-orientation (112–113°) is such that it points straight back at the cursus. While it is conceivable that this could be a coincidence, one suspects that it was deliberate, and that something similar may apply at Maiden Castle as well.

In terms of tornado theory it is easy to conjecture why the alignment of Broadmayne I was arranged. Eye-witnesses might have observed the Sky-God tornado, just after it had created a damage trail on Martin's Down at Long Bredy, traversing Broadmayne minutes later as an overhead funnel cloud. Alternatively the tornado may have made ground contact at Broadmayne as well. In either event, the community at Broadmayne may have wished to memorialise the same Cosmic Consummation by constructing a bank barrow to perpetuate locally the visitation of the Sky God.

At Maiden Castle Mortimer Wheeler's excavations proved that the bank barrow was constructed after the causewayed enclosure had been in use for a long period. Work on it began in the central area and continued westwards as if to direct it towards the cursus, but where it crossed the ditch of the enclosure it was necessary to infill the latter. At this point the direction changed as if to aim more directly at the cursus which was concealed by hills. The finding of 'ox' skulls in the bank-barrow ditch speaks again of the cult of the bull or Sky God, just as cursus-building does. Hence we find in South Dorset and North Dorset, at the two fourth-millennium causewayed enclosures of Maiden Castle and Hambledon Hill, temporal and physical links between enclosure (a social and religious centre) and cursus, the two paired, it would seem, by the long finger of the bank barrow.

From what is known of the archaeology of cursuses, their adoration spanned a thousand years of British prehistory, so it would be surprising if the enormously influential Windmill Hill/Avebury region had not partaken in the religious practice of Cursus God idolatry which everywhere else in Britain was so intense. One need only look at the ancient monuments of the Thames Valley, which at one point passes not far north of the Windmill Hill area, to find that over half a dozen cursuses once existed in the valley between Lechlade and Middlesex. So why was there no ditch-and-bank cursus close to Windmill Hill?

It is worth asking whether the Neolithic megalithic avenue south of Windmill Hill, known as Beckhampton Avenue, was inaugurated for just this purpose. In contrast to the Stonehenge area which was largely barren of good stone, huge sarsen blocks were liberally scattered across the Avebury region. Because a tradition of their use in chambered-barrow building had long existed, the Windmill Hill people may well have translated the cursus concept of parallel banks-and-ditches into stone. The same could be postulated for some of the stone rows of Dartmoor, Exmoor, Wales and Western Scotland and the initial phases of stone-row construction at Carnac, Kerzerho, and elsewhere in France.

Only two stones of Beckhampton Avenue survive, but fortunately many stones of a second avenue, known as the Kennet Avenue, remain (see map on p.190). These megaliths are frequently ordered in pairs of contrasting shapes. There are lozenge-shaped stones which are said to betray female characteristics, and slimmer ones said to be male stones. It is a feature of the hard sandstone blocks known as sarsen stones, or bridestones, that they tend to appear in polygonal form. The lozenge was a symbol of the Goddess Age and stood for the Goddess herself, while the word 'bride', as used in bridestone, may be a reference to the ancient British Goddess Bride, Brigit or Brigid. The ancient Britons chose their megaliths with care. Male stones look slim, while female stones appear polygonal, fatter and often lozenge-like *when viewed along their intended line of sight*—which in the case of avenues would presumably be from a processional viewpoint. In Indonesia and India alleged male stones are often dedicated to a man, and female ones to a woman. If the often-alternating stones of the avenues and circles at Avebury can allow us to judge, then this could imply that the prevalent Goddess-worshipping society maintained a fair balance between the sexes.

Beckhampton Avenue at Avebury is over two kilometres long and, according to Aubrey Burl and others, much older than the Kennet Avenue and the circles. Its sinuous progress bears comparison with the proposed Long Bredy cursus and accords with the facts of tornado theory. The apparent average width of the avenue (16–18 metres) is near the minimum expected for tornado path-lengths of two or three kilometres, so the idea may be put forward that the stone avenue was built to follow a tornado path in order to mark it for eternity. This suggestion overcomes a problem which is otherwise difficult to explain. If the Windmill Hill people wanted to build a ceremonial way lined with megaliths out of free choice, why did they not choose easier ground and avoid the crossing of two water-courses? The engineering problems were already enormous without having to build wooden bridges and drag the gigantic blocks over them as well. One of the bridges had to be twenty metres wide in order to cross the fifteen-metre wide stream, which meant the felling and transportation of huge trees. The problems are such as to suggest that the megalithic avenue builders had no choice regarding the route to follow—it was Divine Providence, in the form of the Tornado-Sky God, that willed it on them.

The age of Beckhampton Avenue is unknown. The finding of a Beaker burial with a vessel of 24th century BC type, buried within a special three-stone setting called the cove, gives us a latest possible date, because it means that the cove is at least this old, but it gives no clue as to how much older the cove might be than the beaker, nor how much older the avenue might be than the cove. All I can say is that, from what we know now, it is quite possible that the first of Avebury's processional megalithic avenues followed the winding trail marked out by a tornado in much the same way that the Calne tornado did on 30 December, 1859 and which also went close to Windmill Hill (Chapter 5). Whereas the few surviving, mostly fallen, megaliths seen by William Stukeley were quite massive, it does not follow that all the avenue stones were huge. The missing stones could have been smaller than the familiar Avebury ones. After all, it would be the smaller stones which would be destroyed first, and the builders of an early, very long cursus-avenue comprising hundreds of stones might have preferred to use comparatively small megaliths to make their work easier, but including occasional exceptions like those at the entrance to the henge and near the Beckhampton Cove. If so, the holes in the underlying chalk would be shallow and hard or impossible to detect by geophysical-survey techniques.

8

The Stonehenge Cursuses

Looking to the north from the stone circles of Stonehenge, it is possible to see part of the 2.7-kilometre long monument that is the Stonehenge Cursus. This is the Greater Cursus, discovered by Dr William Stukeley on 6 August, 1723. But there is a Lesser Cursus as well, which is important both in itself and for several noteworthy, co-existing tornado parallels. Regrettably, the Lesser Cursus has vanished from sight.

Like so many cursuses subjected to centuries of plough action, the banks of the Lesser Cursus have been effaced. Nothing remains today but transient cropmarks which appear over the former ditches during periods of dry weather. But the plough was not entirely responsible for erasing this cursus from the landscape; the main job was done in antiquity by the Neolithic people themselves, who backfilled the ditches not very long after digging them! When the remains of the Lesser Cursus were found by the alert Richard Colt Hoare, 180 years ago, enough was left of the banks for him to identify their positions. Since then the modern plough has removed even these slight traces.

The Lesser Cursus is 400 metres long and 50 metres broad. It lies 650 metres north-west of the western end of the Greater Cursus, two kilometres north-west of Stonehenge. Partial excavation in 1983 by Julian Richards produced helpful finds and evidence to suggest that it was built in two stages. In the first the length was 200 metres, with shallow ditches 30 centimetres deep, ending in the east with a cross-bank. In the second stage the ditches were deepened, and the cursus extended eastwards a further 200 metres, leaving an open end in place of a terminal ditch and bank. Then, soon afterwards, the cursus was closed down and the ditches filled with material from the banks—but leaving enough to survive until the nineteenth century AD, when Richard Colt Hoare spotted what remained.

While it will never be possible to know the full intentions of the builders, we can use the available evidence to suggest what may have happened. The initial size of the cursus and its orientation (from the west-south-west) conform with the straightness and uniform width typical of a short tornado track. Such tracks are easy to follow where they pass through a forest or a stand of trees. The middle cross-bank of the cursus could have marked the point of exit of the

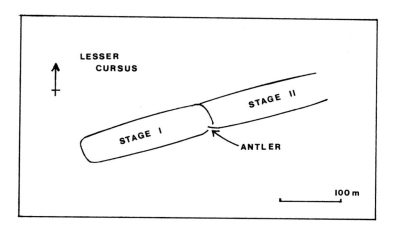

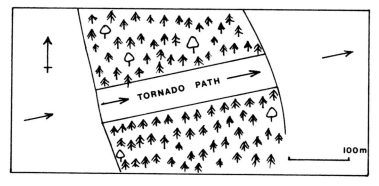

The Lesser Cursus at Stonehenge, and a comparison of its orientation and dimensions with those of the May 1979 tornado which tore a path through a tree plantation a few kilometres away on Ablington Down.

Aerial photograph of the tornado track which cut through the trees of the Ablington Down plantation near Stonehenge in May 1979. *Photo The Salisbury Journal.*

tornado from forest to grassland, after which the devastating wind disappeared across open fields.

This suggestion is no idle speculation. Just such an occurrence took place eight kilometres north-east of Stonehenge at 1320 GMT on 30 May, 1979. The tornado arrived from the west-south-west and destroyed 200 trees over a path fifty metres wide across the entire 300-metre length of the forty-year-old Wig Plantation on Ablington Down, above Figheldean. Because the ends of the track were rectangular where the tornado entered and left the trees, a square-ended enclosure or cursus would have resulted if landscape engineering had been attempted, based on the trail left by the Neolithic Sky God—for this is what appears to have happened in the Age of the Cursus when the cult of the Spiral-Tornado-Bull Cult was rising. For the first time in the locality of the Pre-Stonehenge People, the track left by the Tornado Sky God was to be preserved as a major earthwork. The date was about the middle of the fourth millennium BC, several centuries before the first earth was moved at Stonehenge.

The Lesser Cursus was originally built so far, but it seems that, after only a few months or years, the diminutive cursus was regarded as inadequate for the pride and needs of the community when compared with others in the south of England, particularly the Dorset Cursus. So the Lesser Cursus was deepened and elongated eastwards but left open-ended to indicate that the true length of the path taken by the Sky God was unclear. The tornado of 30 May, 1979, continues to provide the perfect parallel, because we know that it pursued an eastbound course over open country for a further kilometre before catching the tops of the next plantation as it was lifting and dissipating.

For some time the people probably had to be content with this small cursus, for want of anything better, but after some years (as at Rudston, Yorkshire, perhaps) the Sky God returned to mate again with the Goddess.

Striking the plain or forest 650 metres to the south-east, and in full view of eye-witnesses if it was daylight, another spiralling tornado sped eastwards. This more powerful whirlwind, on a slightly different orientation, left a damage track which led to the building of the Greater Cursus. The devout farmers, inspired no doubt by the explanations of a priest or priestess, could now raise a monument truly worthy of the Tornado-Bull-Cult—a grander monument which would compare more favourably with others of which they had heard tell. So at regular intervals along the ditch bottoms of the Lesser Cursus they placed stag-horns and antler tools in ritual and definitive honour to their beloved Sky God. One of these bones provided the material for dating the closure of the cursus to about the middle of the fourth millennium BC or rather later. The ditches were then filled with chalk rubble from the banks of the cursus.

The Greater Cursus, more generally known as the Stonehenge Cursus, is a magnificent spectacle when viewed from either end or from the air. Its west–east orientation is typical of the direction taken by many British tornadoes. The length is 2.7 kilometres and its width, which varies, averages more than 100 metres, with the maximum of 130 metres half-a-kilometre from its western end. The ground undulates gently from the west as the cursus descends into a dry valley and rises again to the opposite terminal. Although the banks are much eroded, especially in the heavily ploughed eastern half, they are easy to follow on both sides of the western section.

It is believed that this cursus dates from at least the beginning of the henge of Stonehenge and probably earlier, in the third quarter of the fourth millennium BC. In fact, there is a high probability that it was founded at the same time that the Lesser Cursus was closed down. The discovery by J. F. S. Stone of a Grooved Ware sherd and of a 90-millimetre piece of Welsh Cosheston-Senni mica-bearing sandstone of Milford Haven type, from the base of the cursus ditch near Fargo plantation at the western terminal, indicates that the cursus was still in use well into the third millennium. Grooved Ware sherds, interred in a ritual pit, were found by William Hawley at the bottom of the ditch encircling Stonehenge, two

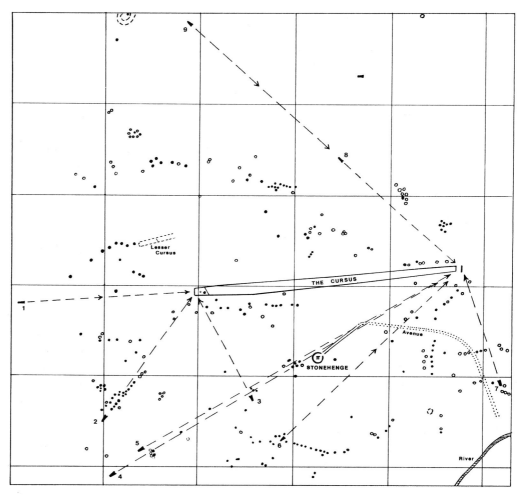

The chief Neolithic and Bronze Age monuments in the neighbourhood of Stonehenge and the cursuses. The nine long barrows which bear on the terminals of the Greater Cursus are numbered in accordance with Table IV. Round barrows are indicated by small closed circles; open circles mark the positions of destroyed barrows. The initials VC pinpoint a large spiral-centred vortex-circle cropmark which formed in July 1990. © *Crown copyright*

adjoining sherds displaying chevrons. This pottery is characteristic of the middle part of the Neolithic era when the Goddess religion was in its ascendancy. Farther to the south-west, in Dorset, Richard Bradley has proved that the Greater Stonehenge Cursus is younger than the immense Dorset Cursus, and the finding of third-millennium Beaker pottery there bears further witness to the long period of use enjoyed by cursuses in Southern England.

Exploratory excavations have been made at both terminal ends of the Stonehenge Cursus by Julian Richards and others. A sample cross-trench was cut through the western terminal in 1987 and half the terminal bank restored to its 1947 condition, before it was damaged during military manoeuvres. The bank outside the eastern end, at right angles to the cursus, which had always been regarded as an 81-metre long barrow (called Amesbury 42) was shown to have been raised by deepening the ditch of the true eastern terminal (since vanished) merely to imitate the mound of a long barrow. The bones of no less than four or five oxen (*Bos longifrons*), uncovered by John Thurnam in 1868, had already hinted at its true identity, 'and there may have been others not reached by the excavations. Altogether, the appearances justify the conclusion that oxen were slaughtered at the time of the obsequies for the funeral feast, and that the heads and feet, not being used for food, were thrown on the yet incomplete barrow, as offerings, to the *manes* or to other deities.'

But there were no Neolithic interments, and no obsequies—because this was no burial barrow. It was part of the cursus, and the offerings could only have been dedicatory ones of the long-horned Neolithic bull. The bank was to honour the Sky God and to serve another purpose too (probably the reason why its height had been raised so effectively)—to provide a better sighting device to allow it to be seen over several kilometres. Much the same can be said for the unobstructed western terminal, whose height enabled it to be seen from afar. The proof lies in the extraordinary series of long-barrow alignments designed into the Stonehenge Cursus landscape.

There are sixteen long barrows within five kilometres of Stonehenge, and scholars have searched in vain for solar or lunar alignments in their orientations. Aubrey Burl states generally that long barrows were sited for the mound to be conspicuous. This is true of a large number of Wessex long barrows, including in the Stonehenge region the equinoctial barrow Figheldean 27 (Knighton Barrow) which is so well exposed on a hilltop three kilometres north-north-east of Stonehenge that it can be seen for very many miles about.

I have surveyed all long barrows in the Stonehenge region in order to gain the highest possible accuracy for their orientations, using a military marching compass accurate to half-a-degree. I was able to establish the orientations of the best preserved barrows with an accuracy of one degree, but for most others, reduced in height and broadened with age, plus or minus (±) two or three degrees was the limit. Where barrows had been nearly obliterated I used probes to locate the positions of the filled ditches, which allowed ranging rods to be set up. It should be noted here that the self-orientations given on large-scale Ordnance

Survey maps are not always reliable. However, although I was unable to determine all axial orientations with great precision, it was possible to measure very precisely the relative orientations between cursus terminals and distant barrows.

With the single exception of the equinoctial barrow Figheldean 27 (Knighton Barrow), *all long barrows within sight of one or other end of the Stonehenge Cursus are aligned on one of the cursus terminals* (See Table IV).

TABLE IV

Alignments between the Stonehenge Cursus and its long barrows

	Barrow Name	Grid Ref	Length metres	Self-orientation	Bearing to terminal
THE LONG BARROWS ORIENTATED ON THE WESTERN TERMINAL					
1	Winterbourne Stoke 53	SU 09174280	32	E c87°	87°
2	Winterbourne Stoke 1	SU 10004151	74	NNE/NE 36°	34.5°
3	Amesbury 14	SU 11544176	31	SSE 154°	153°
THE LONG BARROWS ORIENTATED ON THE EASTERN TERMINAL					
4	Winterbourne Stoke 71	SU 10104090	c50	NE/ENE c58°	58°
5	Wilsford 34	SU 10414118	36	NE/ENE c56°	59°
6	Wilsford 13	SU 11894130	20	NE 44°	44°
7	Amesbury 140	SU 14184194	20	SSE c160°	162°
8	Durrington 24	SU 12474440	44	SE 135°	133°
9	Figheldean 31	SU 10894588	45	SE 135°	133°

NOTES

1   A tenth barrow, Amesbury 10a at SU 11944217 (west of Stonehenge), has been excluded because it is reported that ditches have not been detected on air photographs; however, the barrow is shown on earlier maps as elongated with a self-orientation of 60° which directs it at the eastern terminal's outer bank. So even if it is not a ditched long barrow, this 'long mound' may have been planned into the cursus barrow system.

2   Founder's Barrow. Winterbourne Stoke 1 held the skeleton of an old man (a chief?) with a shaped piece of flint 20 cm long (tornado replica?) at his right arm.

3   The outer bank of the eastern terminal is skewed to 186° compared with a cursus-perpendicular angle of 174°. Can this deliberate skew be a time-of-day indicator for an anniversary date?

4   The azimuths of Durrington 24 and Figheldean 31 as seen from the eastern terminal are close to that of midsummer sunset.

12. The moment of consummation. Divine Union is achieved with the womb
of the Great Goddess.

13. Detumescence. The Marriage of the Gods took place at three minutes after sunrise, when
the phallic shade reached the Goddess Stone, or Womb Stone, through the vulvar arch. Now,
several minutes later, the shadow is noticeably retreating. Photograph taken 19 June 1989.

14. Viewed from near
the top of the Heel Stone,
the shadow is seen reaching
the right-hand side of the
vulvar arch.

15. The whole of the
Heel Stone is visible in
this photograph taken 24
minutes after sunrise on 1
July 1987. Although the day
of the actual Midsummer
Marriage is long past, the
effect of the shadow can
be seen for two weeks after
the solstice, or as early as
two weeks preceding it,
from a position outside
the monument.

This rule applies unreservedly to seven of the long barrows in the table. The second and third barrows (Winterbourne Stoke 1 and Amesbury 14), which are very close to the cursus and accurately aligned upon its western terminal, are just out of view due to small variations in the slope of the land, although the tops of neighbouring trees can today be seen. It can only mean that the nine barrows were built after the event that prompted the building of the cursus, and this must signify that the cursus was the focus of worship. Among these nine barrows the more distant ones were possibly the latest, built after the cursus terminal banks had been heightened. Figheldean 27, exposed on a hilltop in view of the cursus, is close to the ancient Robin Hood's Ball causewayed enclosure. Because this one long barrow in sight of the cursus is not aligned on a terminal it probably predates the cursus. The barrow Bulford 1, which is three kilometres east of the cursus, is excluded from the list because it cannot be seen from the cursus; nor can the equinoctial Wilsford 30 just south of Normanton Down.

A possible solar alignment links Figheldean 21 and Durrington 24 with the eastern end of the cursus. As seen from the northern end of the east-terminal bank the direction of these barrows is 312° to the nearest degree (but 313° when measured from its centre), whereas the prehistoric midsummer sunset azimuth was 311.5° for a view of the last tip of the setting sun's disc.

It is important to realise that the outer bank of the east terminal of the Stonehenge Cursus (formerly known as long barrow Amesbury 42) stands on land about two metres higher in elevation than where the cursus otherwise terminates. The people appear to have found that the cursus track finished inconveniently early and that the eastern terminus, as originally built, was obstructed from the east by the height of the nearby ridge. The objective was to place this additional 'sighting' monument on the brow of the ridge to increase its height and bring it within view of all six of the barrows which point at the eastern terminal.

From the west terminal the long barrow known as Winterbourne Stoke 53 is plainly visible end on. Its orientation is parallel to and aligned with the Stonehenge Cursus. Tornado theory suggests that the barrow was positioned to preserve the azimuthal direction from which the tornado funnel cloud arrived before it struck the ground or forest. This barrow was dug into by William Cunnington in the nineteenth century and found to contain evidence of unusually extensive burning prior to the raising of the mound. This could mean that bonfire beacons or funerary pyres heralded the construction of barrow and cursus, perhaps imitating the tornado funnel itself on anniversary dates.

The other long barrows which are accurately aligned on the western terminal (Winterbourne Stoke 1 and Amesbury 14), despite their closeness are just hidden from it by the brow of a low hill; their precise alignments could have been achieved· with the aid of high posts or fires. The magnificent barrow Winterbourne Stoke 1, 74 metres long and adjacent to the busy A303 trunk road, is still in reasonable condition. It is orientated on a bearing 36 ± 1–1.5°, and not on 41, the most northerly moonrise, as Aubrey Burl suggests in *The Stonehenge People*. In this barrow John Thurnam found what he took to be a phallus of flintstone. It lay close to the right arm of an old man buried at the eastern end with his head to the south-west. John Thurnam described the object as a

The 20-centimetre flint found with a corpse in the Winterbourne Stoke long barrow (long barrow number 2 in Table IV). The shape is both phallic and tornadic. Its position suggested to the excavator that it was a most treasured possession. Did it belong to the man who planned the building of the tornado-made cursus?

'bludgeon-shaped flint about eight inches long, and well adapted for being grasped in the hand. From one end numerous flakes had been knocked off, and it had evidently constituted an object of considerable importance to the owner'. Could this flint have been shaped to be an imitation of the divine phallus—the tornado funnel—of the Sky God, part of the paraphernalia of a religious ceremony connected with the monument? Was its owner the man who masterminded the prestigious cursus operation? Although this long barrow is orientated on the western terminal and not on any cosmically-possible moonrise, the round barrows which sprang up in a line north-east of the long barrow during the next thousand years had a common azimuth around 41°. This is the direction of extreme northerly moonrise as seen from the forecourt of the long barrow looking towards the knoll which constituted the local horizon.

Besides the copious evidence of bull sacrifice in the east-terminal bank of the cursus (the former Amesbury 42 long barrow), the Amesbury 14 long barrow which is aligned on the western terminal yielded the skull and feet of an ox or bull. Apart from the barrows mentioned, no other cursus long barrows have been excavated, but numerous long barrows on the western half of Salisbury Plain (at least six, probably eight) have yielded *Bos longifrons* skulls, hooves and other bones, in addition to the skulls and feet from the mortuary long barrow known as Fussell's Lodge. Richard Colt Hoare, for instance, found seven or eight bull or ox-skulls in Boles Barrow (Heytesbury I). Farther north, towards Avebury, the excavation of a Bronze Age round barrow at Hemp Knoll by M. E. Robertson-Mackay uncovered a grave pit with the complete head and four hooves of an ox (or bull) as an accompaniment to a Bell-Beaker burial. This discovery proves that a form of Bull God worship persisted in Wessex for a very long time because a thousand years separate the building of these long and round barrows. The bovine remains from Hemp Knoll help to emphasise the ritual nature of the findings from the Salisbury Plain long barrows and the Stonehenge Cursus.

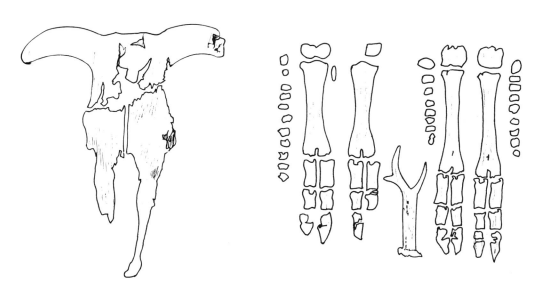

The head and four hooves of a bull which had been ritually buried in a Bronze Age round barrow at Hemp Knoll on the Beckhampton Downs in Wiltshire. A roe-deer antler was also found there.

Contemporary with the bull-cult was the adoption and use of antler symbolism. The association of antlers with fertility aspirations originates in the perennial shedding and 'rebirth' of this hard-wearing material. Its appearance in the ditches of the two Stonehenge Cursuses, in probably most Salisbury Plain earthen long barrows, in the Neolithic circular ditch of Stonehenge and in innumerable Early Bronze Age round barrows bears witness to something more than the carefree abandonment of a well-used tool upon the completion of chalk-ditch cutting. I

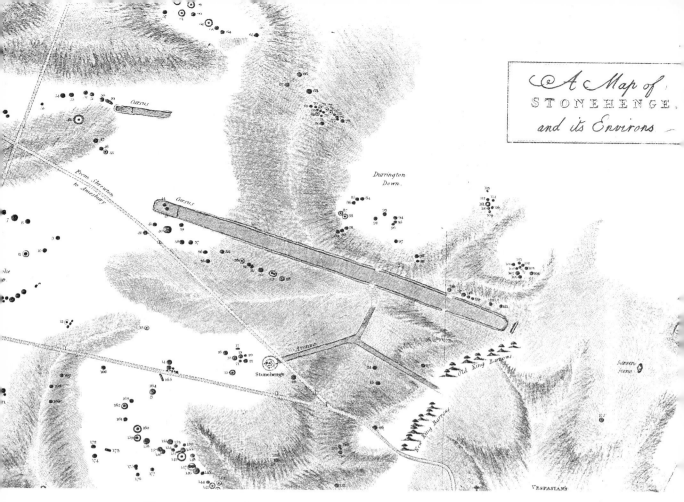

The region of the Stonehenge Cursus drawn by Richard Colt Hoare in the early part of the nineteenth century. The Stonehenge Avenue is shown as having a northern arm but this is due to the misinterpretation of a modern track.

believe that the antler, sometimes worn-out, sometimes virgin, was returned to Earth as a thank-offering to the divinity whose timely loan had eased men's labours, while simultaneously functioning as a fertility and rebirth symbol because of its rapid growth and uterine shape. On certain ceremonial occasions antlers would have served prominently in fertility and funerary rituals, as they still do in surviving folk traditions from our ancient past, such as the annual Horn Dance at Abbots Bromley in Staffordshire, which is held in the first week of September.

Further evidence of the age of the Stonehenge Cursus can be found by examining the reasons for the pair of opposed causeways located about 600 metres from its eastern terminus. William Stukeley and Richard Colt Hoare noticed these gaps in the banks and ditches which can no longer be seen but whose former positions are detectable by probing. When the monument was in use, it was only through these entrances that the interior could be reached without clambering over ditch and bank. Richard Colt Hoare commented that the straight avenue of Stonehenge, leading north-east from Stonehenge and along which midsummer sunrise is seen, is directed at the causewayed gap in the southern bank of the cursus. If this is intentional, what lies behind it?

Firstly, if the causeways consist of uncut chalk this implies that either the cursus and Stonehenge were planned together (circa 3200 BC, this being the approximate date for the circular ditch of Stonehenge) or, because it is unlikely that the circular ditch predates the cursus, the causeways were left as simple entrances to the cursus without knowing that Stonehenge would one day be constructed (the exactness of the alignment is not known). On the other hand, if the causeways are made from rammed chalk, then a connection may lie in the fact that the first Stonehenge postdates the building of the cursus, possibly by a good interval.

Archaeologists have inferred that the long barrows date from the middle or early part of the fourth millennium. In that case, because I have concluded that all nine cursus long barrows were built after the Greater Cursus, the cursus must date from a similar period, and be a few centuries older than the founding of Stonehenge. However, since the date for the closing of the Lesser Cursus may be the middle of the fourth millennium, I suggest that this may date the founding of the Stonehenge Cursus. The nine cursus long barrows would therefore be, at the earliest, contemporary with these events, while some could be later (this would leave only a few non-cursus long barrows, such as Figheldean 27, and the causewayed enclosure of Robin Hood's Ball as being more ancient).

A final question at this stage concerns the length of time that the Stonehenge Cursus remained in use. The fact that J. F. S. Stone found bluestone chippings on the ditch bottom could mean that the chippings got there about 2200 BC when the bluestone circles were being prepared for the centre of Stonehenge. Some belief in the sanctity of the cursus was therefore still alive a thousand years after its inauguration.

*   *   *

Over five thousand years ago in Neolithic times, probably as far back as 3800–3400 BC, prodigious longitudinal monuments were being built across the face of Britain. Over hill and dale, sometimes crossing waterways, they meandered and wound, or went straight as a die. Cursuses are unique to this country. No ditch-and-bank structures of enclosure type, built on such a scale, are known anywhere else in world prehistory; but in Britain, principally in England, several dozen were built, with lengths mostly ranging from one to ten kilometres and breadths chiefly between 40 and 100 metres.

Since the discovery of the first cursus near Stonehenge in the eighteenth century, the cursus enigma has given archaeologists an exceptional and increasingly difficult challenge as the number of known examples has risen. Today, it is clear that, without external aid, archaeological resources alone will be insufficient to resolve the main problem: what sort of stimulus could drive men to desert their farms and pastures and labour for months on end with the idea of scouring deep ditches in chalk or limestone and piling up banks of such colossal length? Added to this are the problems of forest clearance and long-term maintenance.

Although documentary evidence will never be forthcoming, and all knowledge of myths and lore concerning the cursuses vanished thousands of years ago, it is probable that the major force behind cursus building was religion. It has been thought that British Neolithic religion was a realm so dark and remote as to be beyond the reach of any anthropologist or religious historian; nevertheless, I have shown that an interpretation combining religion with meteorology can account for all the major features of the cursuses and can provide a good base for myth-building, too. Such large-scale earthwork construction could scarcely be achieved without the advice and authority of a priest-led or at least priest-assisted powerbase. No shamanic individual or religious community leader or godless chieftain could command the influence that would mobilise the workforce for years or decades at a time. But families of devout, pious farmers would respect the opinions of priests and priestesses who could offer celestial explanations in conformity with prevalent belief, explanations which would not challenge but would sustain the needs of a simple agrarian society.

A universal motif commonplace in primitive mythologies portrays the divine couple Sky and Earth, or Sun and Moon. Appearing at the focus of creation myths, they supply the spiritual understanding of a cosmic scene in which Earth is revered as the mother deity and Sky is the father deity. Their marriage enriches the world and gives birth to all life-forms. The powers of the sky gods originate from their fertilising capacities which they owe to their gift of life-bringing rain. Goddess Earth responds by succouring the seeds and causing them to emerge as grass and cereals. Every rainstorm is a cosmic event welcomed for its life-bearing gifts, but in the thunderstorm is the godhead about which lightning darts and thunderbolts and hailstones scream to the ground. Here is the Sky God in his manifestation of Storm God where he boasts his strength and bellows like a bull. And when he lowers his twisting funnel to the ground—his anticlockwise spiral of destruction—that is when his potency and masculinity are savagely and terrifyingly apparent.

In conspicuous union with Earth he scars the forest and field, and only the Earth Goddess survives the onslaught. Everything else yields to the spiralling wind, and a track of devastation remains for mortals to meditate on. Every community understood the spiritual message; and because each came to desire and expect such a 'visitation from the sky' the religious leaders ensured that the Cosmic Consummation, when it came, would be commemorated by a Cyclopean earth-moving project.

Archaeology dates the chief era of the building and exploitation of cursuses from the second quarter of the fourth millennium to the end of the third millennium—around 1,500 years. An association with Grooved Ware has been found at some cursuses, early henges and stone circles. Aubrey Burl comments that, because Grooved Ware appeared in the context of a new ritual, the ceramic deposits were symbols of a new cult; but he concluded 'we shall never know the ethos of this cult'. The Bull-Sky God cult in connection with the tornado revelation may partly answer this question. More will be inferred in the future by re-analysing the significance of excavated objects and bones in the context of ritual and domestic activity, and I have shown that much can be learnt from studying cursus dimensions, shapes, directional changes, and orientations, and the siting and contents of related, neighbouring monuments. Using a socio-religious approach which includes the role of atmospheric powers in the choreography, a small part of the religious fabric of these ancient times has already been clarified.

The cursus was the creation of the Sky God, a roaring celestial bull with spiralling spout, thunderbolts and hailstones, his worship ritualised through offerings of bull's heads, horns, antlers, phalluses, discs and balls. We can admire a British cursus in its symbolic context and ponder over its spiritual implications. It is the ancient Briton's supreme tribute to the gods, an everlasting memorial to the day they met on earth—an occasion celebrated annually forever after, at the place where the consummation took place. A cursus was a priestly monument, the biggest construction in the Neolithic world dedicated to Divine or Sacred Marriage. Ritual rings of pits and posts, henges and megalithic rings followed afterwards, but all the while the cursuses proclaimed to newcomers the ancient rights to land-use and tenure held by the lineal descendants of the cursus-builders—those ancestors who had witnessed the coming of the Sky God in the remotest past.

William Stukeley's choice of the word *cursus* has proved to be a shrewd and happy one because the ditch-and-banked cursus was, as he guessed, a course or way which must at times have attracted events that assumed a processional character. But the cursus was no secular avenue; it was consecrated to the highest, the most potent divinities of the spiritual world in commemoration of their sacred meeting. The point of entry, the 'landing terminal', was the Gate of the Gods, and the point of departure was a second Gate. Therefore the cursus was the divine way, the Path of the Gods. That same path led me to uncover the secrets of the meaning of Stonehenge in Autumn 1985 when, having solved the relationships between the long barrows and cursuses at Stonehenge and in Dorset, I returned again to that age-old mystery: what was the purpose of Stonehenge? What is its iconography?

9

The Henge of Stonehenge is Born

About the year 1666 John Aubrey wrote in the manuscript of his book *Monumenta Britannica*: 'I am now come to Stone-heng, one of our English Wonders, that hath been the subject of so much Discourse'. Three hundred and twenty-five years later, and through the centuries in between, the discourse has not ceased. Despite considerable advances on the archaeological front the main problems have not been cracked. Why was the monument built? What did it represent? How did it function?

The reason why Stonehenge has not yielded its ultimate secrets is because no one has yet succeeded in reading the minds of those who built it. To decipher the monument, we must restore elements of the lost religion and rediscover the essential myth of the times. I have shown that the prevalent belief centred on a fully fecund female deity, the Great Goddess, and that a crucial component of the mythology was the rite of Sacred or Divine Marriage. Not only did this concept glorify the Goddess to an exceptional degree, but it embraced, to a lesser extent, her marriage partner the Sky God as well.

The great cursus at Stonehenge was still in use when work began on the first Stonehenge. The digging of the circular ditch came first: the purpose was to raise a bank to enclose the sacred area. The ditch was irregular and consisted of short sections which, to judge by their lack of symmetry, seem to have been dug simultaneously by separate gangs and the sections joined by breaking down the intervening walls. We know this from the excavations of William Hawley who spent several seasons at the monument in the 1920s. While it is true that he carried out part of his operation, especially in excavating the eastern half of the monument, with insufficient care (as Mortimer Wheeler put it, his work was done 'like digging up potatoes') and his excavation diaries are incomplete, nevertheless, some of his discoveries are valuable and helpful. Although he never prepared detailed archaeological reports he published annual interim papers, and to this day his diaries remain available at Salisbury Museum for inspection by members of the public.

The beginnings of Stonehenge date from the last quarter of the fourth millennium BC. Carbon testing on three stag-horns from the base of the great circular ditch dates them to around 3200 BC. This corresponds with the digging of the ditch according to both William Hawley and Richard Atkinson because the ditch was never subsequently back-filled; it silted up slowly and naturally over succeeding centuries.

Two causeways were left when digging the ditch: a major one at the north-east in the general direction of midsummer sunrise and a lesser one at the south. The north-east entrance is the ceremonial and holy entrance to the sacred space of the circles. The southern entrance was possibly intended as a secular point of entry, like the back door of a church.

Most of the chalk rubble cast out from the ditch was used to raise a circular bank on its inside, and the diameter of the circle thus defined is 93 metres. A causewayed circular monument of this type, of which there are more than seventy in Britain, is known today as a henge (Stonehenge being the site which gave rise to the name). The most prominent feature at this time was a massive megalith, the Heel Stone, placed outside the bank on the north-east side where it still stands, probably in its original position, for Richard Atkinson and Aubrey Burl are agreed that the Heel Stone was set up at the very birth of the first Stonehenge. A pottery sherd of Windmill Hill type, which is early Neolithic, was found near the bottom of its stone-hole, showing that the Heel Stone corresponded to the oldest period of the monument. The top of this solitary stone is somewhat rounded but it seems that no attempt was ever made to modify its shape, its coarse ruggedness bearing witness only to the repeated onslaught of frost and weather.

Considerable speculation has surrounded the reasons for the choice of the site of Stonehenge, much of it astronomical. It is important to know what constructions were there in the earliest stages. Luckily archaeology has provided us with useful if incomplete clues. If we can decide what was planned into the design at the beginning, we can more aptly pose the question, why?

We can at least be clear on what was there during what Richard Atkinson designated the phase one constructional period, although unfortunately his phase one is a thousand years long! Besides the big bank, ditch and Heel Stone there were at least four megaliths: the two 'station stones' surrounded by their own smaller circular banks and ditches, and two other 'station stones' without ditches. There is excellent evidence for a central structure of wood and there may have been a pair of 'entrance' stones, too. The 56 Aubrey Holes, located a short distance inside the peripheral circular bank and set on a ring 85 metres in diameter, belong to this period as well, but the crucial question is, were they part of the original plan? Aubrey Burl has bravely tackled this problem in his valuable work *The Stonehenge People.*

There seems to be no doubt that the Aubrey Holes were a later addition to the design. Each hole is a pit, about a metre broad and a metre or so deep. All the holes were dug in one go and immediately filled with rammed chalk, after which they were used from time to time over the years to receive cremations and ritual deposits. The contents of thirty-two of the holes were hurriedly examined by William Hawley; two more on the southern side were methodically emptied by Richard Atkinson in the 1950s. Carbon dating of a wood-charcoal deposit proved that their period of use came 500 years after the founding of Stonehenge. These ritual pits had nothing to do with the original purpose of the monument.

So what was at the centre of the great grass-covered circle in its earliest days? Aubrey Burl presents a good case for a circular building made of timber with an inner wall of diameter thirty metres and an outer wall slightly greater than this —about 31 metres. These diameters are only slightly smaller than the diameter of the sarsen stone circle which was raised more than a thousand years afterwards. Several of the holes for the posts which supported the wooden structure have been excavated. One of them had been cut into when a stone-hole was being prepared for Stone 12 of the later sarsen ring, around 2000 BC.

An avenue of posts leading to the wooden edifice from the southern causeway suggests a rear entrance to a twin-walled construction. The size of the main posts of the building can be judged from one of the post-holes into the chalk rock, which was 1.2 metres deep and 0.8 metres across. It had been packed hard with rammed chalk. The result of William Hawley's work led Aubrey Burl to conclude that the building was once thatched and that it had an opening to the north-east and a lesser entrance to the south. The latter was approached by a non-straight wooden passage which may have been roofed. Why was it thought necessary to have the wooden construction facing north-east?

Since the site of Stonehenge is on sloping ground, a more fundamental question is this: why was such an awkward site chosen for consecration? Could it have been the deliberate choice of a priestess or priest for some arbitrary reason that will never be fathomable, or was it a decision dictated by the intervention of some extraordinary circumstance—much as the tornado path ordained the location of the cursus, a site hallowed of itself because it was decided by Nature, otherwise recognised as the Goddess?

In *The Goddess of the Stones* I made out a case for the consecration of circular patches of ground by the Goddess believers of the Neolithic era as the result of natural atmospheric vortex phenomena which leave circular spiral-centred impressions in fields of crops or grass. The scientific background to these vortex phenomena is well documented and is presented in my books *The Circles Effect and its Mysteries* and *Circles from the Sky*. The evidence overwhelmingly supports such a conclusion for those Neolithic stone circles and round barrows for which geometrical testing is possible. Although henges, which served a purpose similar to that of stone circles, do not have such well-defined boundaries as the stones of the stone circles, their similarity of shape and overlapping chronology suggest a similar origin, at least for some of the smaller, earlier, circular henges. What are the chances that this happened at the birth of the henge of Stonehenge?

Firstly, the region is known for the occurrence of natural vortex-circles. I have examined a number of cases of this uncommon phenomenon in the last ten years on or close to Salisbury Plain. Secondly, the dimensions which apply to the timber-post circle of the original Stonehenge correspond with dimensions typical of the bigger circles which scientists have been studying. In the 1980s some of the largest vortex-circles had diameters of 30–31 metres. Another big circle, which was not surveyed, was kept under observation during the four seconds that it took to form. In broad daylight on 3 July 1982 it appeared in a cereal field some 250 metres from the observer at Westbury, Wiltshire, just below the northern escarpment of Salisbury Plain. The diameter was estimated as 30–35 metres, and the formation of the circle was accompanied by the hissing sound often made by natural air-vortices like whirlwinds.

The similarity of these dimensions to that of the fourth-millennium beginnings of Stonehenge is remarkable. The link between the repetitive 30–31 metre natural circles and 30–31 metre Neolithic buildings is dramatic, for, besides Stonehenge, a 30-metre diameter timber structure is known to have existed inside Durrington Walls, a henge of much later date which encloses part of a dry valley near Stonehenge. At the valley bottom, in a position where, occasionally, crop circles develop in similar locations, there are the remains of a 30-metre round building whose post-holes were uncovered by Geoffrey Wainwright twenty years ago. From this one might infer that the enormous henge of Durrington Walls was built to enclose an area where crop circles occurred, and that timber structures were raised on at least one of the natural circles. Another timber edifice in the Durrington valley had a diameter of nearly 15 metres which is also

A natural vortex circle formed by the action of a spinning volume of air.

a commonly-recurring crop-circle dimension. I am not stating that Stonehenge *was* founded in this way, merely that it might have been.

It is therefore possible that at Stonehenge the people found a circle, in a crop or in long grass, and saw it as a holy directive to dedicate a temple at that spot. Maybe witnesses were close by when the event took place. Farmers have always made the maximum use of daylight; they would have been up and about in the early hours, the time when many vortex-circle systems form. They may have heard the noise of the spinning air which is a typical whirlwind sound, humming, screeching or throbbing. Perhaps they *saw* it happen, the crop or grass bending before the vortex, the spiral pattern manifesting itself as they watched! Throughout Britain and Ireland the spiral sign and spiral-circle centre were already well-loved symbols with powerful Goddess associations, in which the spiral centre was thought to be the opening to the Goddess's womb. The mystical thinking was that the Goddess opened Her womb for the benefit of humankind.

How best might the occasion be used for the good of their tribe and heirs? With the hindsight of five thousand years, I suggest that the answer was to build a monumental structure upon the circle-site in order to memorialise the occasion with anniversary and seasonal rituals. The monument could take the form of a wooden structure 30–31 metres in diameter at the centre of a circular bank of earth and chalk rubble laid out as a 93-metre ring. The purpose of the bank was to mark off the area of sanctity; the outer ditch served simply as a quarry for the contents of the bank.

The creation of the circle could be interpreted as a moment of marriage, a fleeting union between Goddess Earth and phallic vortex, the aerial spirit which spins out the circle and creates the place where God and Goddess mate in cosmic matrimony.

Such a site—the centre of the resulting circle—might be viewed as an eminently suitable meeting place for spirits, or as a site for communication with the Great Goddess in Her tripartite role as Goddess of the Underworld and Earth, Goddess of the Waters, and Goddess of the Moon and Heaven. In any event, a decision was made to set the central temple facing the rising point of the midsummer sun, for the sun was the ever-present masculine deity of the sky.

For this purpose, and with annual ceremonies in prospect, a north-eastern causeway was left in the bedrock when the chalk was being chipped away to make the ditch. The circle is most likely to have been formed in late May, June, July or August, the months when the majority of the circles appear, and the likelihood that it formed in standing grass intended for haymaking favours the period late May to June. Whether or not the midsummer festival was nigh, a link was established between the infant henge and the midsummer sunrise. A sarsen stone with a rounded top was located outside the gleaming white chalk bank in the general direction of midsummer sunrise. It would help if we knew what it was called—perhaps it was the equivalent of Sun Stone or Shadow Stone, Phallus Stone or Stone of Life—but for the last three hundred years it has been known as the Heel Stone.

The essential elements of the scenario are complete. The sun rises on midsummer morning at its most northerly point along the eastern horizon, shines upon the open north-eastern side of the timber shrine or temple, and illuminates its interior. The waiting faithful would know that all was well with the world, that the season was on time, that midsummer's day had arrived. The full significance of this spectacle is considerable and is explained in the next chapter, but there are major questions to discuss first.

Although the Heel Stone nearly corresponds with the point of midsummer sunrise five thousand years ago, in a direction which is rather less than 50 degrees east of north, it is positioned on the right-hand side of the causewayed approach as seen from the centre of Stonehenge. The main breadth of the causeway is well to the north of what one might expect, the axis directed at 46° 33′ from north. Why should this be? One possibility was to allow the approach of a procession from a direction which would not interfere with celestial happenings along the sacred midsummer axis. But it is also possible that the causeway was skewed in order to permit the light of the moon, when rising at its extreme northerly point of its 18-year cycle, to radiate along the causeway towards the central monument. Aubrey Burl discusses this fully in *The Stonehenge People*. However, the skew is not exact, probably because the moon was not rising at its most northerly point in the year when the chalk was being split and lifted from the ditch.

My suggestion that the siting of the first Stonehenge arose by chance explains the long-standing puzzle regarding its rather poor location. The ground is neither

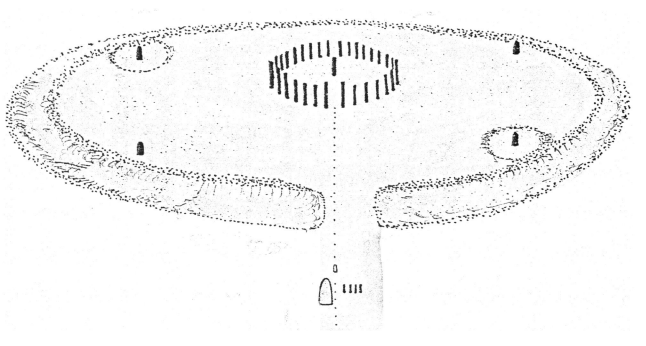

The first phase of the circular henge of Stonehenge, begun about 3200 BC. There was a wooden structure at the centre, perhaps a simple ring of posts at first or the elements of a more substantial building. The Heel Stone lay at the extreme edge of the chalk causeway which was aligned on neither the midsummer-sunrise axis nor a major lunar axis, but was broad enough to allow observance of both solar and lunar risings at the most northerly parts of their cycles.

flat nor high. A place a couple of hundred metres away would have greatly improved the general aspect towards the horizon. From Stonehenge the ground slopes into a shallow, dry valley which is often mist-filled around dawn in quiet, fine weather, even in midsummer. The slope was sharp enough to pose construction problems for the wooden building which, on the basis of the post-hole sizes and their arrangement, some archaeologists believe was roofed. Aubrey Burl's suggestion, that the site had the advantage of being approximately midway with respect to the cursus and that the whole of the cursus could be seen from it, is an excellent one, although, as he says, if these were the only objectives, a small shift of the site would have improved its location still more. A few hundred metres to the north the land is level, higher, and the cursus can still be seen. Dr Burl's opinion is that a location midway along the cursus was the deciding factor, although if this is so its misalignment of 75 metres from the cursus centre amounts to an error of 75 metres in the cursus half-length (one half of 2774 metres), which is four per cent. If exactness had been important, the mistake was needless because the Neolithic people could survey much better than this when they wished. More relevant is the fact that the midsummer orientation from Stonehenge is not directed towards any obvious part of the cursus.

Despite cursus and henge being contemporary, and although they both glorify the sexuality of the Goddess, the site of Stonehenge was not chosen to orientate the Heel Stone on either terminal of the cursus. On the other hand, it is curious that the Stonehenge alignment is apparently directed towards the only known causeway in the southern side of the cursus. This cannot be seen today, but Richard Colt Hoare sketched the cursus with its break in the southern bank before nineteenth-century ploughing erased it. The causeway is known only from probing, not from excavation, so we do not know if it consists of uncut chalk or rammed chalk rubble, the result of a later infilling operation. As I have not probed for the cursus causeway, the sketch of Richard Colt Hoare is all we have to go on, so we cannot be sure whether the alignment which is apparent in his published sketch is exact. But if it is, and if it turns out that the cursus causeway consists of rammed chalk, then we know that its linear alignment with Stonehenge was a deliberate late amendment. If it is made of uncut chalk, then a degree of pre-planning could be indicated. It might mean either that the cursus and henge were designed together, or that the site of the henge was intentionally aligned on the earlier cursus causeway. This would reduce the possibility that the location of the henge was dictated by the random arrival of a vortex on the hillslope. Whatever the case, whether a vortex was involved or not, the main argument is unaffected. The intention when digging the earthen circle at Stonehenge was to enclose sacred space.

The principal feature of Stonehenge at this time was the midsummer alignment of the Heel Stone with the henge centre. Every June the sun returned, and the orientation re-created its effect. The midsummer celebration was an annual affair which must have brought joy to the hard-pressed peoples of those times. I do not take the view that Stonehenge was a gloomy place, built with a central mortuary house and intended mainly for funeral processions. However, there may well have been a charnel house of some sort at the henge centre at some period, or even at the outset. But if the dead were left to rot in the central building as Aubrey Burl suggests, then it is more likely that they were there for the purpose of being reborn. Dr Burl stresses the importance of the moon and its motions, and in this context one should note that near the Heel Stone there are post-holes suggesting that at some stage the directions of the rising moon were being monitored. Astronomically the argument is valid, but we must remember that the moon moves in an 18.6-year cycle with regard to its rising and setting directions. Only in every nineteenth year would the moon rise at its most northerly point and in the Age of Stonehenge lives were short; few people survived beyond the age of thirty to forty. For much of their short lives the Stonehenge people had no extreme northerly moonrise to witness, but the sun kept returning, shining past the Heel Stone at every midsummer festival. So it is more probable that the purpose of the henge, even in its earliest days, was to exploit the activity of the sun which contributed to a festive ritual every June, an event of truly cosmic importance which brought security and happiness to a hard-working community.

10

The Marvel of the Stonehenge Alignment

For a thousand years Stonehenge maintained its stoneless centre. The few stones at the site occupied peripheral positions near the bank and ditch. Only from about 2200 BC, near the start of the Bronze Age, were there stones in the central area, and it was only about 2000 BC that the great sarsens arrived.

These are the stones first noticed by visitors as they approach the monument on Salisbury Plain. At first appearing small in the distance, they vanish from view as the approaching traveller drops beneath the low hill. Then, as the stones come into sight again, they loom from the landscape grandly and impressively, and this time the solitary Heel Stone beyond the main group to the north-east is easily seen, too. Among these great stones are the small bluestones from Wales, which remain scarcely visible until the visitor is almost on top of the monument.

The stones of Stonehenge have been much disturbed. Some are broken, many are missing, and most others are pitted or damaged by the passage of time. There was a melancholy period when visitors to Stonehenge took hammers with them, or hired them from Amesbury, that they might remove a piece of stone for themselves; and it is likely that bits of broken stone from the monument lie sadly in walls or gardens or beneath the metalled road which runs so hideously close by it.

It is worth looking at a plan of the stones as they lie now, together with the

Stonehenge from the Amesbury road, an etching published in 1812 by Richard Colt Hoare in *The Ancient History of Wiltshire.*

banks of 3200 BC and the start of the midsummer-sunrise avenue built about 2200 BC, in comparison with a reconstruction which shows the arrangement at the end of the final stone-moving phase, about 1550 BC. After this date, we know from archaeological evidence that the only noteworthy work relevant to the monument was the two-kilometre extension to the avenue which until then had been limited to a single straight section 520 metres long and twelve metres wide. This continuation to the river was effected several centuries after the stones had been brought to Stonehenge and, despite the long interval that had elapsed since then, may have been made to follow the route of the stone-hauling teams. Excavations in the ditches of the western extension near West Amesbury produced antlers for radiocarbon dating. One indicated a date of about 1345 BC (based on a radiocarbon assay which gave 1070 ± 180 b.c.) and the other, some distance away, gave about 975 BC (800 ± 100 b.c.) These dates confirm that, although the heyday of the Stonehenge period was past, the Age of Stonehenge continued until about the end of the second millennium BC. Until this extension of the avenue was constructed the north-eastern end had remained open, pointing in the direction of both the midsummer sunrise and the only gap in the southern side of the cursus.

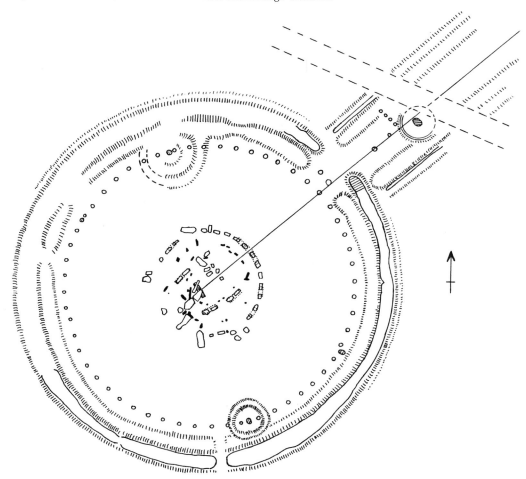

Stonehenge as it is now, with many central stones damaged, fallen or missing. Shaded are the Heel Stone, the Altar Stone and the four peripheral 'station stones'. The filled-in part of the surrounding ditch at the entrance causeway is also shaded.

The stones lie in the centre of the area enclosed by the circular bank and external ditch, still with its original diameter of 93 metres. Measured across its outer edge, the diameter of the stone circle is nearly 32 metres, a little more than the 30–31 metres of the former wooden structure. The north-east causeway links the stones of the central area with the straight earth-banked avenue. A thousand years earlier the axis of the causeway had been 46° 33', but when the avenue was built and made to align with the midsummer sunrise the axis was modified to agree with both, namely 49° 54' 40".

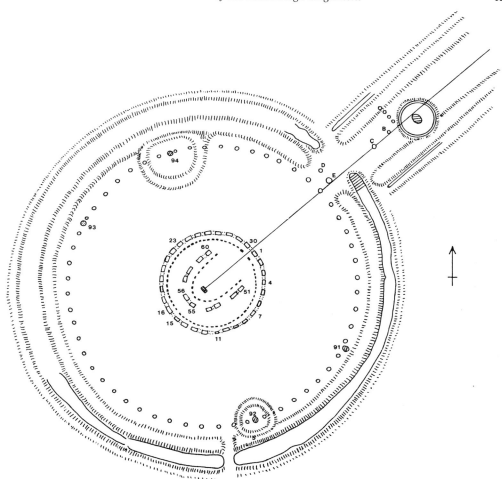

Stonehenge with the central stones in their final arrangement, about 1550 BC, but with the visible earthworks (the banks and ditches) shown largely as they are now. The positions of the 56 Aubrey Holes are indicated but not the Y and Z holes.

The innermost sanctum is formed into the shape of an open-ended ellipse, or horseshoe, by the arrangement of five trilithon arches axially aligned on the midsummer sunrise. They are sarsen, a sandstone harder than granite, brought at least thirty kilometres from the region between Avebury and Marlborough in the north of Wiltshire. These stones are graded in height so that the biggest pair of upright stones, one weighing fifty tonnes and towering almost seven metres above ground level, forms the apex of the horseshoe which is completed by two opposing pairs of stones of lesser but equal height, the shortest being at the

The one stone still standing of the mighty great trilithon. At 6.7 metres high with a 23-centimetre tenon on top, only the Rudston Monolith in Yorkshire is taller in Britain. When the lintel was in place the trilithon rose to a height of 7.4 metres.

The trilithon with dagger carvings towards the base of the left-hand stone, illuminated by the summer evening sunshine.

The Altar Stone, which I believe to be a Goddess Stone, lies recumbent and buried—pressed into the ground by the weight of the stones of the great trilithon which felled it.

Side view of the Heel Stone, showing the extent to which it is leaning from the vertical.

horseshoe tips. Including the thickness of the lintel, the height of the great trilithon is 7.4 metres, which compares with 6.2 metres for the shortest of the trilithons.

This arrangement provides an imposing backdrop for what is the focus of the entire edifice—the Altar Stone. This stone, which used to be the most splendid of all the megaliths, was misnamed in the seventeenth century by the fancy of Inigo Jones who is best remembered for his inaccurate drawings and wishful reconstruction of the monument. The Altar Stone lies sadly prone, broken and largely hidden by the fall of the lintel and one upright of the great trilithon. To make matters worse, the great weight of the stones lying on it has pushed it deeply into the ground so that only its upper surface can be seen today. But at one time this stone rose proudly three metres high, and stood perpendicular to the solar axis four metres in front of the great trilithon that was later to destroy it. The Altar Stone is one of Stonehenge's foreign stones, made of a fine-grained, pale-green mica-bearing sandstone from the Cosheston Beds that jut into the coast of Milford Haven in south-west Wales, nearly 300 kilometres distant. When scraped, microscopic mica mirrors are exposed which make the rock glint in the sunshine. This raises the first of two major questions which have to be resolved by anyone seeking to explain the iconography of Stonehenge: Why should this particular type of stone, from so far away, have been selected for the focal position of the Bronze Age masterwork?

Including the Welsh Altar Stone, there were formerly some eighty stones at Stonehenge which were alien to the county of Wiltshire. These were the bluestones, all unquestionably of Welsh origin and whose hue 'mystically' deepens when wetted. In their final settings they occupied two groups—one a carefully composed horseshoe of nineteen stones within the great trilithon group, the other a rather hastily-erected circle of sixty bluestones between the great trilithons and the outer ring of lintelled sarsens. But long before this reconstruction took place, around 1550 BC, the bluestones had stood elsewhere in Stonehenge's sanctuary, and it was for that purpose that they had originally been brought there around 2200 BC.

The outer ring of sarsen stones, those first seen by today's visitors as they approach the monument, consists of thirty upright 26-tonne stones with thirty lintels forming a perfect circle. Although the site on which Stonehenge was built slopes towards the east, nevertheless the heights of the outer-ring uprights were so arranged that the lintelled circumference was almost precisely level. The diameter of this outer ring of stones is about one third of the overall diameter of the site.

Beyond the circular bank and ditch remains that primitive and basic feature of the monument, the rugged, isolated Heel Stone. An explanation for its shape and position is crucial if the riddle of Stonehenge is to be solved. During thousands of years of weathering it has acquired a cracked, uneven surface, but its general outline is much the same as when it was first put into use around 3200 BC. Nonetheless, one far-reaching change has taken place, and that has been a progressive tilting away from the vertical, for the stone now leans markedly towards the monument.

If, as Richard Atkinson and Aubrey Burl believe, the Heel Stone has not been dressed, we may safely assume that it was carefully selected for its size and shape. Its present height is close to 4.7 metres, but restored to the vertical the apex would rise an additional 0.5 metre. From a ground-level width of 2.4 metres, as seen from the south-west, the stone slowly tapers until near the top it becomes quite rounded. Viewed from the centre of Stonehenge the shape is so obviously phallic that, despite a lack of any clear evidence of phallic worship at this place, this aspect has been commented upon from time to time.

Perhaps because so much has been written about the importance of sunrise alignments at Stonehenge, most people are surprised to learn that the Heel Stone does *not* point to the rising of the midsummer sun, nor could it ever have done so in any past age. As an astronomical indicator the Heel Stone direction is no better than an approximate marker.

Today, if one watches the midsummer sunrise from a position standing on the main axis in front of the Altar Stone and looking directly up the avenue—that is, straight through the centre of the trilithon arch—the Heel Stone is not cen-

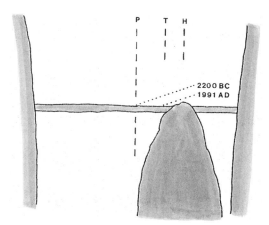

The leaning Heel Stone as seen from the Altar Stone today by an observer whose eye level is about 1.55 metres above present ground level. P marks the direction of the prehistoric sunrise for about 2200 BC, T gives the direction of sunrise today, and H is the Heel Stone direction. The course followed by the upper limb of the sun is indicated for 2200 BC and the present day.

trally framed within the arch as most photographers of the midsummer sunrise
would have it appear. Furthermore, the tip of the sun shows to the left of the
stone, and then passes to the right as the full orb comes into view. Because the
Heel Stone protrudes so little above the tree-covered horizon, the sun is not
much obstructed by the stone as it goes past (at most by ten per cent). It is at
this moment that most photographers take their pictures.

There are several reasons why this view of the midsummer sunrise differs from
what used to be seen in the Age of Stonehenge, the most obvious being caused
by the present-day slant of the Heel Stone. To correct for this, in makeshift
fashion, the modern observer and photographer may try crouching or sitting
instead, because this has the effect of raising the apparent elevation of the apex
of the Heel Stone as seen from the centre of the monument. This explains why,
since 1986, I have taken to lying or sitting with my camera at the centre of
Stonehenge facing the midsummer sunrise. From this position, whereas the solar
apex still comes into sight just to the left of the Heel Stone, the sun now goes
wholly out of sight behind the stone rather than passing close to its top. A proper
allowance for the inclination of the Heel Stone from the vertical is obviously
needed, but the choreography is also confused by the important fact that in
prehistoric times the midsummer sun did not rise where it does today.

At the midsummer solstice the sun now rises in a direction of nearly half a
degree to the north of the Heel Stone's azimuth (50° 54′), but in the Age of
Stonehenge it rose even farther to the north than that. The azimuthal drift of

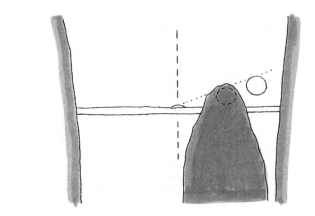

Revised sketch demonstrating the effect of straightening up the Heel Stone. This is
approximately how the Heel Stone would have appeared to a prehistoric observer from a position
in front of the Altar Stone. Shortly after sunrise at the midsummer solstice the sun would
be eclipsed as it passed behind the Heel Stone.

the point of the midsummer sunrise eastwards along the horizon results from an astronomical effect called the precession of the equinoxes. Since the year 2000 BC this has affected the position of sunrise by rather more than a solar diameter, the rate of movement along the horizon amounting to about 0.2 of a degree every thousand years.

On the other hand, within the limits of measurable accuracy we know that the axis of Stonehenge is aligned with the axis of the Stonehenge Avenue (49° 54′ 40″), which itself corresponds to the prehistoric solsticial sunrise for the end of the third millennium BC, if one supposes that the horizon was tree-covered as it is now. The Heel Stone's position is to one side of this common axis. Therefore an observer at the centre of Stonehenge, at the time when the monument was designed and built, must have seen the sun rising freely over the tree-lined horizon, unaligned with and unobstructed by the Heel Stone.

The second fundamental question to be answered, then, is why did the designers and worshippers not bother to fix the Heel Stone precisely on the Stonehenge/Avenue/sunrise axis if it was the axis that was so supremely important? Can it be true, as some investigators have suggested, that the later builders were content with the relatively crude positioning which their ancestors had seemingly accepted?

Aubrey Burl has tried to answer this by suggesting that around 3200 BC, at the founding of the earliest Stonehenge, when the peripheral banks and ditches were made and the axial direction of the north-east causeway was set at 46° 33′, it was sufficient that the bearing of the Heel Stone should only approximate to midsummer sunrise, although the Heel Stone was over one degree east of the 3200 BC sunrise and the causeway was as much as three degrees north. This, he claims, was because it was the moon, not the sun, that was of primary interest. Following John Edwin Wood, he pursues the idea that the Heel Stone had been located about midway between maximum northerly moonrise (40–41°) and minimum northerly moonrise (60–61°) in order to signal about four or five years in advance when measurements of the direction of the extreme northerly moonrise should commence (the two extremes being separated by an interval equal to half 18.6 years). In those early days, before the orientation of the causeway was modified, the Heel Stone stood on the right side of the causeway and the most northerly moonrise lay in the direction of the left side. So it could be thought that the builders intended by their action to get both lunar and solar events into the scenario.

Yet the basic problem has been dodged, not answered. Why should the planners be so careless about fixing the solar direction when it was extremely easy to be exact about it? More pertinently, why was the misalignment of the Heel Stone with the solstice, if that is what it was, not corrected, either when the

Awaiting the Midsummer Marriage. The Heel Stone projects above the horizon, as it was intended to do when positioned by the Stonehenge People. A jackdaw perches on top as the moment of sunrise approaches.

Welsh bluestones came to Stonehenge, about 2200 BC, or at a later date when the mighty sarsens were delivered? If more than a million and a half man-hours could go into rebuilding the monument, why was not a single day spent heaving the Heel Stone a couple of metres north-westwards? This point is crucial and must be explained by anyone seeking to explain the riddle of Stonehenge.

No answer has ever been forthcoming, and yet it is really very simple. The Heel Stone was not moved *because it was already in the right place*! From the moment it was set in its present stone-hole it has been achieving exactly what it was intended to do. And the secret of that vanished with the death of the last of the worshippers at Stonehenge some three thousand years ago. The reason why the Heel Stone had to be located east of the midsummer sunrise position answers a very basic question relating to the primary motives behind the erection of the monument that is Stonehenge.

The non-alignment of the Heel Stone with the midsummer sunrise is instantly explicable if it is supposed that the intention was to observe the actual rising of the sun followed by its immediate eclipse by the same stone. The builders either worked this out exactly before settling on the position of the Heel Stone or they arrived at the intended arrangement after trial and error, during which the stone temporarily occupied holes other than its present one. It can certainly be no accident that the Heel Stone is exactly the right size and is at just the right distance beyond the circular earthwork to throw its round-topped shadow to the heart of the monument.

It is unfortunate for the modern observer that after so many centuries the Heel Stone is leaning badly from the vertical. It is essential to determine the apparent elevation of the vertical Heel Stone just as it was in prehistoric times when the stone circles were prepared. In 2200 BC (the date of the first bluestone rings) it would have been 5.2 metres tall. Clearly, the height to which the sun becomes concealed by the stone is appreciable but it is not so much the view of the sun relative to the Heel Stone which is important; the crucial point is to what extent the Altar Stone gets subjected to shade. Therefore, inverting the procedure and looking at the situation from the opposite direction—that is, by considering what happens at the Altar Stone itself, we find by comparing relative heights of Heel Stone and Altar Stone that a shadow at least 1.25 metres high cast by a vertical Heel Stone falls upon the three-metre high Altar Stone.

We also need to consider any effects that might result from the chemical solution of the sub-soil chalk rock by the flow of percolating rainwater during the course of four thousand years. Richard Atkinson estimates a lowering of 0.54 metres (although I have reason to believe that this is too much), combined with a surface level change of five millimetres caused by recent soil and turf level movements. Nevertheless, whatever the solution rate may reasonably be, I doubt whether it could lead to any significant difference in the amount by which the Altar Stone gets shadow-covered, for there will be no significant relative change of height between Heel Stone and Altar Stone anyway. The three-metre high stone will still have its lower part in shadow while the upper part remains in the sunshine. We can therefore reconstruct the prehistoric arrangement of sun and Heel Stone at sunrise on midsummer's morning, as it was intended by the bluestone-ring builders about 2200 BC and the sarsen-ring builders about 2000 to 1500 BC. Their aim was to have the sun wholly eclipsed by the Heel Stone shortly after an unimpeded sunrise. This is what I call the 'eclipse trick'.

It is the key to the solution of Stonehenge.

We may at any rate be sure that at *all* times since work on Stonehenge began in 3200 BC the shadow of the Heel Stone has reached to the centre of the monument on midsummer morning, and that since 2200 BC, when the Altar Stone arrived, the lower half of this vertical stone has been shadow-covered as well. Despite the thousands of drawings and models in reconstructions of Stonehenge that have been made, which show the stone lying horizontally, it was never intended to lie flat as an Altar Stone would. It was positioned vertically so that the shade of the Heel Stone should fall upon it.

Because the Heel Stone has probably been in its present stone-hole since the founding of the original henge, it looks as though the eclipse trick was designed into the primordial fourth-millennium phase of Stonehenge when, as Aubrey Burl has so persuasively argued, a stoneless centre was occupied by a timber construction, open to the north-east but with a back-door entrance from the south, the two entrances being in line respectively with the north-eastern and southern causeways. Whether the building was a charnel house or Goddess shrine (perhaps with a north-east entrance similar to those of chambered barrows), the same argument holds. The skulls of bulls, oxen 'or other beasts' found in the central area in 1620 are the offerings of a society with beliefs in a bull-cult. That the people of the age were engaged in the cult of this animal is quite clear because of the great number of long barrows which conceal dedicatory offerings of the heads of bulls or oxen or the antlers of stags, besides which of course there is the unequivocal evidence of the cursuses. As we have seen, the cult of the bull is manifestly interwoven with the worship of both Great Goddess and Sky God, the horned bull providing the communicating link between heaven and earth and aiding the dead on their journey to the Other World. The bull's head and the stag's horns are not dismal signs of the dead but staunch images of hope and rebirth due to their well-recognised uterine symbolism within the context of a Goddess-centred religion.

So whatever structure was at the centre of Stonehenge at its beginnings around 3200 BC, whether shrine or charnel house for the dead, it must have been a focus for prayer and devotion, as well as for the light of the midsummer rising sun— except that it had been arranged that this light was very soon extinguished by the eclipsing Heel Stone. This post-sunrise eclipsing alignment, built into the first Stonehenge of 3200 BC, was retained when the bluestones came to Stonehenge about a thousand years afterwards. In fact, the bluestone people were so satisfied with the old position of the Heel Stone that they dug a circular ring around it to emphasise its sanctity and to distance the profane. The date of this ditch is established by the excavations of Richard Atkinson, as is that of the Avenue; both underscore the solar fixation of the temple and maintain the link with the cursus. With the eighty or so bluestones came the gigantic Welsh Altar Stone with its glittering mica platelets, and this megalith was given the place of honour in the middle of Stonehenge, on the axis of the monument a little to the south-west of centre at what would have been viewed as the Centre of the World. From this moment onwards the Altar Stone became the most important of all the internal stones, even after the later arrival of the 75 great sarsens when Stonehenge was rebuilt in the decades around 2000 BC. The bluestone circles of

16. The bluestones inside the outer vulvar entrance of the sarsen circle emphasise the vaginal approach to the inner womb.

17. The remaining stones of the cove in the northern circle at Avebury henge. The Goddess Stone is on the left and one of her phallic consorts on the right. The midsummer sun rises over Hackpen Hill three kilometres to the north-east beyond the trees.

18. The instant of midsummer sunrise when the sun peeks over Hackpen Hill to produce the Midsummer Marriage at the cove. Photographed 15 June 1986.

19. Avebury s Goddess Stone turns red in the early morning sunshine, and the author's shadow, like that of the phallic shade from stone F, is cast upon it. Photographed 15 June 1986.

2200 BC were in fact never finished. They came down because a more grandiose scheme was to be started. The enormous trilithons went up, the position of the Altar Stone was shifted only slightly along the axis, and the outer ring of sarsens followed, joined to each other by touching lintels. All the time, the Heel Stone stayed where it was—locked in the perfect eclipsing position.

The reason for the special selection of the Altar Stone—which is in effect a Goddess Stone—and for bringing it so far from Wales, is due to its singular quality that when it is freshly scraped and washed its myriads of tiny mirrors shine red in the light of the rising sun—until the reflected rays are visibly extinguished by the advancing shadow of the Heel Stone. Because of the weakness of the solar rays at sunrise this optical trick allowed the arrival of the shadow to be more readily watched. This answers the basic question raised earlier as to why such an exceptional piece of rock should be brought so far for this unique location.

At sunrise the sun at first illuminates the entire stone. Then the shadow arrives and spreads across its bottom half, leaving the upper part in the sunlight.

While a large number of spectators, their backs to the sun, could have been viewing this miracle of optics from within the holy of holies, only very few of the other privileged attendants could have been in a position to watch the sun vanishing behind the vertical Heel Stone. They would have seen the sun's full diameter disappear, only to reappear after an interval of two or three minutes or so (depending on the height of the observer). But this was not so important as watching the Altar Stone glinting in the rising sun, and then seeing its lower half darken as the phallic shade encroached, before glowing again in the sunlight. The supreme climax had come and gone.

About 1550 BC the smaller bluestones, whose positions had been changed on previous occasions, were spaced about in their final order in the middle of the circles. The inner sanctum was crowded with stones and starved of light from the horizons. Although open to the sky, the broad sarsens dimmed the field of vision and created a certain gloom. There were so many stones, bluestones included, that for much of the year light from the rising sun could not get past them. But the light that brought Stonehenge to life suddenly arrived on midsummer morning when the gaps came straight and then the sun at last met the Altar Stone face to face. This central trilithon gap was wider than all the rest, purpose-made to let the sun shine through. And yet so quickly afterwards the shutter closed as the eclipse took place and sent piercing shade into the womb that was Stonehenge. The golden orb, rising clear of the Heel Stone on midsummer's day and shining through the central trilithon gap of the sarsen ring, met its Goddess icon and illuminated the Altar Stone before the extinguishing eclipse replaced sacred light with shadowed union. The stone was not only at the Centre of the World, in the usual religious sense, *it was also at the centre-back of the womb.* The horseshoe arrangement of great trilithons duplicated the human womb, and the Altar Stone was the Womb Stone!

The spectacle was a necessary reminder of the community's origins at the beginning of time, when life began. Of necessity it was transitory and a deeply moving religious experience for the participants. As Mircea Eliade wrote in *The Quest*, this would be a supreme example of 'the profane being transmuted into the sacred by the dialectics of hierophany', that is by the logic of revelation. Just as the belief of the faithful can turn wine into blood, so can similar spiritual logic turn, as here, a stone into a deity.

11

The Marriage is Consummated

It is an epic stage-set. The visual display is exquisitely and sensitively composed, one which every onlooker could readily appreciate.

The underlying myth is that of the Marriage of the Gods, known also as the divine hierogamy—proof that the architects of Stonehenge believed in the creation myth, at one time so widespread throughout the archaic world, of union between Sky and Earth, or Sun and Moon, or Sky-Father and Great Goddess. It is the classic encounter between complementary opposites meeting in union, that supreme moment at the beginning of time when the world was created.

Hierogamy was a symbolical, dramatic episode in the calendar of agrarian peoples. In so many other cultures of the past, known to us through sagas, poetry, folklore and later historical sources, the Sacred or Divine Marriage was a rite, associated with New Year, spring or summer festivals, which involved the ritual mating of people who for the purpose of the ceremony represented the gods. The rite's common, universal objective was to ensure the fertility and productivity of women, animals, and crops. In her study of the Neolithic goddesses and gods of south-east Europe Marija Gimbutas discusses the archaeological evidence for fertility worship and provides solid evidence that the principles of ritual Divine Marriage in south-east Europe are unlikely to have commenced later than about 6500 BC.

At Stonehenge we find the Divine Wedding rendered as a dramatic spectacle

MAUREEN OLIVER 199.

Artist's impression of the Marriage of the Gods. Stonehenge comes to life at the annual wedding of the Goddess with the Sky God on midsummer day—the only time of the year when the phallic shadow of the Heel Stone can penetrate the vulvar gate and reach the centre of the womb.

delicately pictured in timeless stone and moving shade. It is a marriage between images, transfigured and glorified as a marriage between gods.

Every summer on the day when the rising sun arrived at its most northerly point along the horizon the Rite of the Divine Marriage was celebrated as a formal re-enactment of Divine Union. It was solemnly performed in the traditions of the ancestors by an expectant, grateful people wishing to guarantee the safety of their world and the fertility of their crops. Viewed thus, the myth and ritual of the Hierogamy provided a model of their universe. What was for so many archaic societies, elsewhere and in future ages, and not least in south-east Europe, Crete, Greece, and the Middle East, a priestly rite richly embroidered in myth and ritual, was at Stonehenge transformed into a beauteous vision through the performance of the stones.

In discussing the dramatic viewpoint of early societies Joseph Campbell said that in the theatrical drama-logic of religious festivals the cult object is identifiable at least for the duration of the rites with the divinity.

And so it is with Stonehenge.

At the culminating moment, just after sunrise, the Heel Stone eclipses the sun. The shadow crosses the Womb Stone (formerly known as the Altar Stone, but which I shall henceforth call by this more appropriate name) and consummates the ritual marriage on the very day that the sun's power is greatest.

But this is no ordinary stone, and certainly not an 'altar stone' either. The receptive stone is tall and graceful; it stands at the centre of the Spiritual World, on the vertical axis that unites Heaven and Earth, and which traverses and sustains the world. In the mythology of the times its shape—the extended rectangle—related as it is to the lozenge, was viewed anthropomorphically because of its links with the form and attraction of the feminine forces of nature. This stone is the core element of the Goddess, a manifestation of the Earth Mother, like the entire construction about her. The stone circles and horseshoes, with medial passage and gaps, represent womb, vagina and vulva, just as a thousand years earlier the white outer bank of Stonehenge (then two metres or more in height) with its stoneless, wooden centre, may have betokened womb or abdominal wall. The correlation is with door/hole symbolism in which the meaning is identical whether between door and hole, or between causewayed-entrance and Womb Stone, or between circumference and centre. All are feminine images and symbols, the door giving access to the hole.

So we can understand why Stonehenge *is* what it means, because Stonehenge stands, in Old English, for stone 'hanging'—that is, stones 'supported in the air'. The 'entry-passage' stones, numbers 1 and 30 in the general plan shown on p.149, were necessarily vested with a hanging stone—the horizontal lintel which completed the trilithon—in order to present the womb-opening as a true hole to guarantee the most effective spectacle. The concept was then continued all round the circle to meet the demands of symmetry and beauty. It is the lintelled sarsens—the hanging stones, their purpose justified by hole symbolism—that make sarsen Stonehenge the unique megalithic spectacle that everyone knows. At the same time there is another important feature of the trilithon principle—the statement of the three-stone combination by which is proclaimed the *divine* triplicity of the triple-function goddess. Marija Gimbutas summarises the position of threefold symbolism in *The Language of the Goddess*. She records the antiquity of the triple Goddess principle by its appearance in a Magdalenian context at the Abri du Roc aux Sorciers, Angles-sur-Anglin, France, where there is a relief of three enormous female presences with exposed vulvas. Divine triplicity in one form or another is easily traceable in all prehistoric and classical

The Heel Stone shadow on 23 June 1988, photographed from directly in front of the Heel Stone a few minutes after the Cosmic Consummation. The phallic shadow is already withdrawing from its union with the Goddess.

religions, right through to Irish Newgrange, Celtic triple Brigit, Greek Moirai and Roman triple *Matres* (or *Matronae*).

Viewed as a whole, Stonehenge was not just a temple to the Goddess; it *was* the Goddess, and it remains the ancient Goddess to this day!

And the Heel Stone is phallic after all, which explains why it was set beyond the henge bank, clear of the Goddess's abdomen. The idea was divine coitus *and* impregnation. For just as in India, where a tree's shadow was once understood to have fertilising powers, so at Stonehenge a similar function was probably assigned to the ejaculating shade of the Heel Stone. This idea is further supported by the phenomenon of detumescence which watchers could contemplate from outside the henge bank. After observing the ritual marriage by the conjunction of phallic shade with vaginal entrance in the sarsen wall, worshippers could watch the physical detumescence of the shadow after the wedding. The dramatic spectacle, until then restricted to perhaps a couple of dozen devotees inside the stone circles, could now be seen by hundreds more from without. In fact, those attending outside were treated to an equally stimulating and more prolonged pageant than observers remaining inside. A truly practical purpose for the Heel Stone's sacred circle now becomes evident, because by avoiding the sanctity of the little circle, the watchers and their long shadows would not obstruct the miracle of the shadowgraph.

This magnificent spectacle, the Coitus of the Gods, as viewed from outside the temple, continues to this day. It can be followed by anyone who stands on the path next to where the Heel Stone is situated, and I have studied the phenomenon myself every summer since 1986. In the first minutes after sunrise the mating spectacle is seen—the shadow entering the middle trilithon archway —after which, for an hour or so, the detumescence can be watched. This central trilithon archway is the only trilithon which lets the light of the rising sun reach the Womb Stone; it is the only trilithon arch which lets through the shadow of the Heel Stone; *it is the vulva of the Goddess*. To view the spectacle, one stands with one's back to the sun. Everyone who has gone to Stonehenge in midsummer week has stood in the wrong place and looked the wrong way, and they have restricted themselves—unnecessarily—to one day only, 21 June, as though that used to be the only admissible day for celebration.

What are the best days for viewing this grand spectacle? For people watching from outside the monument the answer is some ten days before and after 21 June—the day most people think of as the longest day, the day when the sun arrives at its most northerly point along the horizon. But in some years 20 or 22 June is as long or longer. Data for 1991 show 21 and 22 June as identical to within a second, while for 1992 the 20th and 21st are similarly alike. Neither is there much difference between these three dates for the solar rising position, as the azimuths in Table V confirm. This table also shows that the dates of the earliest rising and the latest setting of the sun (17 and 25 June respectively) are well removed from the date of midsummer's day. For people observing from the Womb Stone at the centre of Stonehenge, although the sun's extreme point of rising to the left of the Heel Stone occurs at the solstice, there is no significant difference between 20 and 22 June, and probably not enough to matter for 19 and 23 June either. Even for 24–25 June (as for 17–18) the difference may not have unduly bothered the gathered assembly if poor weather denied them a viewing opportunity on the best dates; but other dates for this inside-viewing position are less good, perhaps unacceptable, because the sun does not rise clear of the Heel Stone before being eclipsed by it. Of course this may not have ruled them out if continued cloudy weather delayed the Sacred Marriage spectacle day after day. The point is that, although 20–22 June is the target period, depending on the weather, the priests or priestesses might have announced the day of the Marriage festival to be nigh on any day from, say, 17 June onwards. Indeed, for all we can tell, the summer festival

TABLE V

Stonehenge: azimuth, midsummer sunrise and sunset times for a horizon altitude of 0.5°

Date	Azimuth	Sunrise	Sunset	Length of Day
June 15	50.46	3 h 56.16	20 h 19.68	16 h 23.52 min
June 16	50.38	3 h 56.10	20 h 20.14	16 h 24.04 min
June 17	50.32	3 h 56.08	20 h 20.55	16 h 24.47 min
June 18	50.27	3 h 56.12	20 h 20.91	16 h 24.79 min
June 19	50.23	3 h 56.20	20 h 21.23	16 h 25.03 min
June 20	50.211	3 h 56.35	20 h 21.50	16 h 25.15 min
June 21	**50.201**	3 h 56.53	20 h 21.72	**16 h 25.19 min**
June 22	50.205	3 h 56.75	20 h 21.89	16 h 25.14 min
June 23	50.22	3 h 57.01	20 h 22.01	16 h 25.00 min
June 24	50.25	3 h 57.33	20 h 22.08	16 h 24.75 min
June 25	50.29	3 h 57.71	20 h 22.10	16 h 24.39 min
June 26	50.35	3 h 58.12	20 h 22.07	16 h 23.95 min

NOTES: The calculations were done at the author's request by Dr Bernard D. Yallop for June 1989, using the Stonehenge latitude of 51 degrees 11 minutes north, longitude 1 degree 51 minutes west, for apparent horizon altitudes of 0, 0.5, 0.6 and 1.0 degrees. Only the figures for 0.5 degrees are reproduced here. The exact elevation of the horizon in 2000 BC is uncertain because the extent of tree-cover is not known; an elevation of 0.6 degrees may be preferable. Sunrise times refer to the first gleam of the sun, and sunset times to the last gleam. As no allowance has been made for refraction and parallax, the times are to be used only for purposes of intercomparison between one another.

This information is reproduced with permission from data supplied by the Science and Engineering Research Council.

may have spread over several days. As regards the best period for watching the movement of the Heel Stone shadow from outside the monument, there is even more leeway. Although the shadow only penetrates the trilithon womb-opening from 12–30 June, a passable though incomplete impression of the action of the mating shadow can still be gained by attending any of the sunrises from 9 June to 3 July. The drama is at its best, of course, when the sun rises bright and clear in a cloudless sky. The shadows are then sharp and the spectacle sensational.

The statement of symbolical divine marriage, as a re-enactment of the mythical core-element of the dramas of creation of life and the universe, is overwhelming. In so many primitive mythologies there is a quasi-universal theme that, subsequent to the primaeval separation of Heaven and Earth, chaos reigned until cohesion was restored by re-uniting the gods at the beginning of mortal time. The Marriage of the Gods at Stonehenge could be regarded as a living myth, in which the solsticial stage-set combined the community's vivid mythology with the eternal crisis of the renewal of life. If we can judge from what is known of the hierogamy in other agricultural communities, we may understand how these rites concerned people's desires for prosperity by their appeal not only for a regularity of the crop cycle and an abundant harvest but for the fertility of animal stock and the fecundity of humans. That is to say, the rite of Sacred Marriage was an impassioned prayer for the constancy of the cyclic rhythm of existence.

Hence, the Marriage of the Gods made sense of the central mystery that tormented agrarian societies. It provided a rational explanation for the periodical renewal of the world and the harmonious cycle of life, death and rebirth, which embraced planting, seed growth and the birth, death and resurrection of mankind. Stonehenge was a replica of the universe in microcosm. The midsummer marriage was a repetition of the Creation in an intelligible, memorable and inspiring form.

And it was the creation of the cursus that gave birth to the idea; the scheme was to transmute into stone the Consummation of the Cursus.

The Cursus of the Gods was created from a single union of the Sky God with the Great Goddess; and Stonehenge was devised to harmonise and function with the cursus. Aubrey Burl pointed out that the first Stonehenge, of the fourth millennium BC, was sited fairly centrally on a slope so that the entire cursus could be seen from it; and, as he acknowledged, the sole causeway in the south side of the cursus seems to point back to Stonehenge along the line of sight of midsummer sunrise (in which direction the avenue was to be constructed a thousand years later). These, among others (such as the chance arrival of vortex circles), can be considered as potential reasons for the choice of site for Stonehenge. At the summer solstice the rising sun shines down the Stonehenge Avenue, uniting Cursus and Henge along open causeways. The divine influence of the Sky God's cursus was directed to the ritual centre of the henge.

We should here recall that the meteorological origin of the Cursus emanated from the potency of the long, dark tornado cloud and its union with Earth. In the choreography of Stonehenge the Heel Stone's long, dark shadow traverses the ground and kisses the Womb Stone of the Goddess. In shape the shadow resembles the spiralling tornado cloud, because it too is long, slender, and cone-shaped. The old, spiralling whirlwind traditions of the fourth-millennium Cursus were carried forth to the second millennium Stonehenge—but now the stones provided the conjugal meeting place where the Divine Powers were to serve the needs of the community. The Womb Stone of the Goddess is the key to understanding the agrarian Goddess of the Stonehenge drama. In the stoneless centre of the earlier, simpler henge a totem of wood, or other construction, could have served this purpose, but a thousand years later a replacement was sought in lasting mineral.

If she is Goddess of Earth, then in the mythology of the times she is likely to have been Goddess of the Moon and Heaven as well, and the substantial evidence for lunar observance at the henge is not inconsistent with this. The horned head of the bull, often considered in other well-researched cultures to be an animal manifestation of the Great Goddess (besides, of course, the Sky God), bore lunar rights and qualities through its symbolic resemblance with the horned moon. Although the choreography was different at Knossos, some of the Stonehenge practices or sentiments may have resembled the Cretan rites of Divine Marriage between Zeus and Hera. At Knossos this was celebrated in a mythological framework which A. B. Cook has analysed to show the Sun-Bull united with Moon-Cow. The ox-skulls, the horn cores, and the antler horns, deposited in cursus and henge ditches, barrows, and henge centres may have had a functional correspondence with the Minoan horns of consecration; they are at any rate clear proof of an Ancient British bull-cult. In fact, in Minoan and Mycenean belief they were symbols of the Great Goddess, not a patriarchal deity, and in Ancient Britain too there is reason to link the early stage of the bull-cult with matriarchal as well as patriarchal features.

I may add that, of the early cremations deposited in Aubrey Holes, only one (hole 55) had any object interred with it. This hole, which was on a north-east bearing, received two antlers, an offering that would seem to be dedicatory because of its firm fertility overtones aimed at the lunar Goddess. Later, about 2200 BC, part of the ditch near the east side of the causeway was filled with rammed chalk-rubble and the axis of the causeway modified. This signalled that the bluestones and the future Womb Stone of the Goddess were coming to the henge.

12

Goddesses of Stone

The megalith chosen to be the Womb Stone at Stonehenge came from the Cosheston rocks of the South Wales coast, and was selected because of its mica content. It would have been erected before its bluestone companions, otherwise it would not have got through the circles planned to surround it. This pale-green mineral with its flakes of mica sparkles in the sunlight when freshly scraped and wetted. Could any knowledge of this, an annual rasping and wetting, have survived as a folk memory from the last days of Stonehenge, around 1000 BC, to the time of Geoffrey of Monmouth, about AD 1138? Geoffrey was the mediaeval historian who wrote of the curative powers of the stones when drenched with water, and, still later, in 1707, the Reverend James Brome reported that 'if the stones be rubbed, or scraped, and water thrown upon the scrapings, they will (some say) heal any green wound, or old sore.'

Aubrey Burl suggests that the Altar Stone (the stone I call the Womb Stone of the Goddess) may have functioned, as in Brittany, as a 'guardian goddess', a protectress of the spirits of the dead, and he suggested that the stone axe found at its base proclaims its role as the 'guardian of the dead'. In Anglesey, at the Goddess temple of Bryn Celli Dhu, the free-standing pillar stone inside the womb-chamber may have functioned as the central Goddess idol. The free-standing white stone in the interior of Cairn L on the Loughcrew Hills in Ireland could have been specially regarded as a Goddess icon too. At Ty-Ar-Boudiquet in Finistère the comparison with Stonehenge is striking. This V-shaped passage grave faces the midwinter sunrise, at which time the rising sun enters the chamber and illuminates a free-standing megalith nine metres inside the passage. This stone, which is certainly the local Goddess idol, awaits her annual winter visit from the sun.

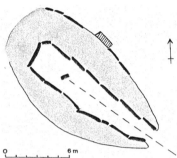

Ty-ar-Boudiquet in Brittany, one of the French sites where the Marriage of the Gods was ritualised in stone. The free-standing megalith in the womb of the Goddess monument receives the seminating sunlight at midwinter, the start of the New Year.

Inside Ty-ar-Boudiquet. Some of the horizontal capstones are now missing, and the Goddess Stone can be seen inside, awaiting the midwinter sunrise.

At Stonehenge no attempt was made to give the Womb Stone of the Goddess any human-related features. Formless but symbolic, the Stonehenge image was potent and efficient as it was. In any case human indications were inappropriate because the stone was not so much the Goddess as a stone within her womb, albeit the principal stone of the womb. It signified, nevertheless, the cult deity about which the elaborate ritual choreography was devised. Stonehenge was therefore a temple in even the narrowest sense of the definition required by religious historians who hold that a true temple accommodates an icon of the deity about which the cult is centred. At Stonehenge, not only does this apply, but the whole structure was designed to represent the deity.

The Womb Stone of the goddess temple rose about the year 2200 BC, but work on the erection of the bluestone circles in their symbolic womb-pattern, begun at the same time, was never completed. As the bluestones went up, it seems to have been thought that the overall operation was insufficient to realise the potentialities of the site. The work was halted, the bluestones were taken down, and the exercise restarted with the audacious sarsen scheme that is Stonehenge as we know it. For about two centuries the eighty bluestones had to be 'stored' somewhere. Perhaps they were set up as a ring nearby, as Rodney Castleden suggests, although it is hard to imagine such a sacred circle, once re-erected, willingly being removed afterwards. Instead, I suggest they may have acted as temporary sentinel guards lining the straight avenue running north-east from Stonehenge. This avenue was built roughly at a time that would make this theory possible. In fact, there is recent evidence by geophysical testing to suggest that stones once followed both sides of the earthen avenue. Whatever happened to the bluestones in between, they eventually reached their final positions lining the Womb of Stonehenge, where they expressed fertility and virility in a pattern of male-type and female-type stones.

Likenesses of Neolithic goddesses in stone or wood are rare in ancient Britain. No megaliths have been so sculpted on the British mainland. Symbolic representations are more common, as I have discussed in *The Goddess of the Stones*. In northern France Goddess Stones are more easily recognised as such because a limited degree of carving was performed on many. Typical from Neolithic Brittany are partly-tooled menhirs with well-developed shoulders and indications of a neck. The standing stones at Medréac exemplify this. On the Isle of Man a splendid stone of this type stands at Cashtal-yn-Ard chambered tomb. We may be sure about the intentions of those who sculpted such works because of numerous anthropomorphic carvings found on tomb-slabs in Brittany where gracefully-chiselled breasts, necklaces and sometimes arms on necked and shouldered outlines were sometimes added. The megalithic engravings at the Allée Couverte of Prajou Menhir (Côte-du-Nord) are distinctive, as are the Déesse

A splendid stone of shining calcite at Médreac in Brittany, the top roughly hewn into the 'head-and-shoulders' so typical of Neolithic Goddess icons in Ancient France. Other megaliths in stone rows nearby show similar treatment.

A carving of four breasts—two small and two big—which may represent the Goddess before and after pregnancy. These are at Prajou Menhir, an *allée couverte* in the Côte du Nord, Brittany, another Goddess monument. Neolithic breast carvings are found at many megalithic tumuli in France.

A Goddess Stone from Laniscar, Finistère, identifable by its shouldered neck, breasts and necklace.

Mère statue from the Island of Guernsey and the sculpture from Laniscar (Finistère) which present the theme in three dimensions.

These carvings are called to mind at Stonehenge by the engraving on the inside of one of the vertical stones of the fourth great trilithon (stone 57). This design has affinities with Goddess representations from Brittany, as Aubrey Burl has strongly advocated, and I agree that it is certainly a Stonehenge Goddess icon. Its simplicity of outline belies the effort that went into executing it, because the large area indicated was wholly hammered out in relief. This elementary piece of art depicting a female deity from the second millennium BC was set on the left (that is, to the west) of the Womb Stone. There is a second engraving, less clear, on the same surface, and another on a nearby lintel.

Opposite, across the sacred space of the inner sanctum, on the inside face of

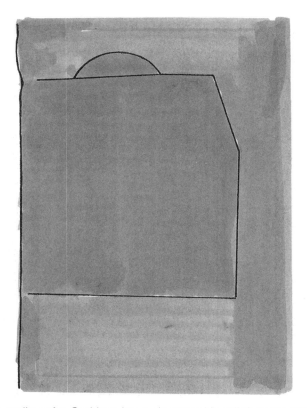

At Stonehenge this outline of a Goddess image is carved in relief on the inside of the western trilithon arch nearest the Goddess Womb Stone (Altar Stone). It measures 1.1 metres high by one metre broad.

a trilithon stone to the right of the Womb Stone (that is, to its east), are the well-publicised Bronze-Age dagger carvings. Again, I agree with Aubrey Burl that they may symbolise the protective abilities of the Great Goddess, so despite being on the right-hand side and of Bronze Age date, they are unlikely to denote the power of some male warrior divinity. A second link with the Goddess is more acceptable because the habitual V-shape of axe and dagger provides an ancient symbolic link with the female triangle and vulva. Like the Breton Goddess whose Goddess stones so often bear axe carvings, the Goddess is here rendered as the Great Protectress.

Stones which are said to exhibit masculine or feminine propensities are commonly encountered in Neolithic and Bronze Age monuments. There are some at Stonehenge. The best surviving pair is positioned just inside the outer sarsen

The dagger carvings on the trilithon stone to the east of the Goddess Womb Stone (Altar Stone). The carvings are about 30 centimetres in length. A photograph of the whole stone is on p. 151.

circle on either side of the principal trilithon entrance—the womb-opening of the Goddess—so that the light of the rising sun, soon to be supplanted by phallic shade, passes between them at midsummer.

Stones are assigned masculine attributes when they are obviously phallic in shape, or appear so when regarded from the intended viewing direction. Femininity is assigned to broader stones, especially those with rhomboid, rectangular, or lozenge-like characteristics. Many examples are known from Avebury and other ancient centres of worship, including megalithic chambered tombs. The lozenge form is typical of the feminine stones at Avebury.

Sexuality symbolised in stone has been affirmed through drawing unambiguous comparisons with explicit carvings which bear sexual characteristics, or because of obvious fertility associations with stone balls, phalluses, and cups. One of the chalk balls from the Neolithic phase of Stonehenge was found in a deposit in the outer ditch, as was a female cup made from a block of chalk. William Hawley's discovery of a perforated disc and ball in the outer ditch may be similarly explained.

A lozenge stone twinned with a male stone, one of many such pairs in the Kennet Avenue at Avebury. Photograph taken at midwinter sunset on 22 December 1985.

Objects like these have been found at other Neolithic sites. Some well-polished stone balls from the Grooved Ware period at Skara Brae in the Orkneys bore spiral carvings as a plain indicator of their role in life-producing rituals. William Hawley's chalk ball from Stonehenge lay close to 'the horn-core of a large bovine animal, having the appearance of a bison'. The probability that masculine fertility symbolism was intended is reinforced by Hawley's subsequent finding together of 'a small horn core of a young bison and two roughly round objects of cut chalk, perhaps intended for balls'. Hollow horn cores have been found in use more recently among primitive societies around the world, sometimes functioning as penis protectors at circumcision and other rituals.

In *The Goddess of the Stones* I showed how the universal symbolism of the lozenge represents the Great Goddess. This comes about as an extension of vulvar symbolism via the principle that the part stands for the whole. A chalk plaque from a ritual pit at Stonehenge Bottom carries a repetitive multi-lozenge pattern which strikingly resembles a similarly engraved stone from the Grooved Ware village of Skara Brae in the Orkneys. At first the lozenge symbol seems

Two tablets carved from chalk, found in a ritual pit close to Stonehenge. In different ways both patterns express vulvar symbolism. Because every trilithon, real or drawn, can now be recognised as a Goddess symbol, opposed triple trilithons produce an even more potent vulvar image, as on the left tablet, particularly the middle pair. The second tablet conveys the same message by diagonal grooves which criss-cross to create Goddess lozenges similar to those found in Scottish and Irish tumuli. These are plainly sacred tablets of a Goddess-worshipping society.

to have expressed, either chiefly or entirely, the fertility aspirations of the artist and worshipper; later it came to symbolise the Goddess. In a still later epoch, I believe that the meaning broadened and the lozenge came to stand for any divinity, male or female, until it was eventually taken over in the Christian era as a celestial designation for Christ himself.

Among the gold regalia retrieved from the rich burial of a chieftain in the round barrow near Stonehenge known as Bush Barrow were two splendid gold objects delicately inscribed with repeating lozenge patterns. This barrow is part of a cemetery on Normanton Down, in full view of Stonehenge two kilometres away. Whatever purpose the objects served, the patterning is typical of the Neolithic and Bronze Age periods and tells us that the deceased person in Bush Barrow held an eminent post in sacred or high office in a Goddess-based religion, the religion of sarsen Stonehenge at the time of its construction.

At various times additional stones have stood in the region of the main cause-wayed entrance to Stonehenge. This is known from the discovery of vacant stone-holes during the 1922 excavations of William Hawley, and the 1979 discovery of Michael Pitts. There is also John Aubrey's plan of the monument which shows three sarsens nearer to the circles than the Heel Stone. The one surviving stone, fallen and misshapen, is a dressed stone which in the eighteenth

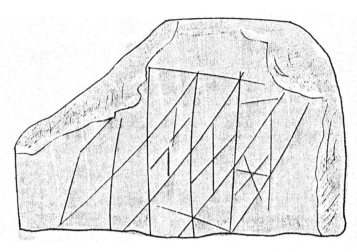

Sacred Goddess lozenges and grooves inscribed on the smooth face of a stone tablet from Skara Brae in the Orkneys.

A well-patterned array of Goddess lozenges decorating a gold object 180 millimetres long—the accompaniment of a rich burial beneath Bush Barrow, a bowl barrow near Stonehenge.

century acquired the undeserved title of 'Slaughter Stone'. If it formerly belonged to stone-hole E (see plan, p.149), it may have been one of a pair of portal stones, neither of which could have interfered with the primary function of the Heel Stone which was to cast its shadow through the middle trilithon gate —the vulva of the monument—to the sanctuary of the Goddess's womb.

Whether or not this proposal is true, there is no doubt that the large stone-hole E which the Slaughter Stone may have occupied was filled in antiquity! This must mean that the stone either fell accidentally some time during the Bronze Age, or was deliberately felled as no longer required; and that in what may have been a more dissolute interlude than the earlier enthusiastic sarsen stone-raising period, instead of removing it, an attempt was made to dispose of the unwanted stone by sinking it into a pit. Otherwise, the great effort that was certainly expended trying to bury this great stone has never been satisfactorily explained. The 1922 excavator of this area of Stonehenge, William Hawley, certainly believed that the Slaughter Stone was felled in antiquity.

In 1666 John Aubrey recorded three stones at this entrance to Stonehenge. He gives no on-site sketch of what he saw but reproduces a plan of the whole monument. Unfortunately the plan was a 'reconstruction' of the temple so one cannot use it to tell which stones were standing, fallen or missing. By 1719, when William Stukeley came to Stonehenge, only the recumbent Slaughter Stone was at the entrance. Most commentators have assumed that the three stones were portal stones and that they were *standing*, an idea initiated by the untrustworthy Inigo Jones who, influenced by Roman temple design, postulated three entrances at 120-degree intervals, each with four stones ('absolutely false,' said John Aubrey) and six great trilithons in place of five. Yet there is no proof that Inigo Jones saw any stones *standing* at the north-east entrance and it may have been a desire for symmetry that made him guess four rather than three. So, of the three noted by Aubrey, one would be the half-buried Slaughter Stone, and a second may have been its languishing partner. What was the third stone?

Whether fallen or standing, but more likely the former, it was probably the stone which once occupied stone-hole C (see p.149). Unlike E, this is not a big hole, which suggests that the missing stone was considerably less massive than, for instance, the Heel Stone. Because its orientation corresponds with the axis of Stonehenge for that part of the second millennium when the sarsen circles were completed, it seems that the stone's function was to point to the midsummer sunrise—although because of its size it did not protrude above the horizon as the Heel Stone did. It seems probable, therefore, that stone-hole B, whose direction from the centre of Stonehenge was slightly farther to the north, had been in use in an earlier age when sunrise was in that direction. One may assume that stone B was taken down, as being in the way, when work on the avenue began and the sarsens started arriving. When the new circles were complete stone B was restored, but since the inclination of the ecliptic and the azimuth of sunrise had shifted since the founding of the henge more than a thousand years earlier, the opportunity was taken to modify the stone's alignment. Accordingly, the stone was moved from B to C, and at some time later it came down. None of these stones would have interfered with the momentous job assigned to the Heel Stone.

The symbolic image behind the iconography of Stonehenge through its rite of the Marriage of the Gods can be regarded as an integration of the sexes. It signifies the generating power of the universe in the absence of which continuous creation would stop. Such images have occupied the minds of farming peoples from the most ancient of days to the most recent of centuries, and an accessible and rich supply can be found in the mythologies of the American Indians. A petroglyph from Spook's Canyon, California, graphically portrays the Sun mat-

A rock carving from Spook's Canyon in southern California showing the sun's rays entering the Earth Mother's labyrinth at the time of the wedding of the Sky God with the Goddess.

ing with the Earth Mother, her womb symbolised by a complex labyrinth. Such imagery recalls the spiritual significance of solar-orientated long barrows in Britain. So many of these fourth-millennium constructions face directions between south-east and north-east that they, too, strongly suggest a Divine Marriage between the rays of the rising sun and the Earth Mother's womb. The forecourt entrance to the chambered barrow or passage grave is modelled on the womb-opening which leads to a vault or chamber, the place of rebirth or regeneration for the souls of the dead. Among the many dozens of tumuli to which this could apply there is the well-known Stoney Littleton (which faces south-east), Newgrange (south-east), East Kennet (south-east), Wayland's Smithy (south-east), Hetty Pegler's Tump (east-south-east), West Kennet (east), Knowth (east), Nympsfield (east), Bryn Celli Dhu (north-east), and Avening Court (north-east). A few, like Dowth at midwinter and Cashtal-yn-Ard at the equinox, have sunset alignments instead.

Another American Indian rock carving is a vivid creation petroglyph from the Iroquois of Tennessee. Here the Sun God's phallus and Earth Mother's vulva are accompanied by an abstract symbol meaning 'to do' or 'to make', which adds power to the symbolic insemination. The Earth Mother's womb, represented by a five-fold spiral, was described by the Potowatomi medicine-priest interpreter

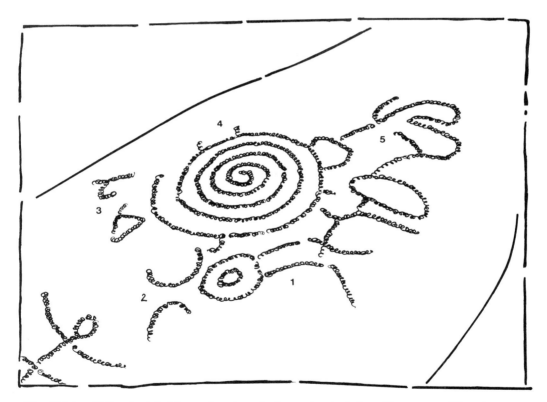

The Origin of Life, depicted in an American Indian petroglyph from Tennessee. The elements are (1) the Sun God's phallus; (2) the Earth Goddess's vulva; (3) the verb *to do* or *to make*; (4) the Goddess's womb of generation, and (5) the subsequent offspring (the Vine of Progeny). Located in the corner on the left is the spiritual guardian.

as a 'coiled serpent or labyrinth symbol expressing the idea that children or young exist in the womb-world fastened together as on a vine or cord'. The Earth Mother's 'Vine of Progeny' issues from the womb and loops back to the phallus and vulva, completing an endless cycle of creation. The whole is watched over by the guardian or priest. It is remarkable how the primary elements of this composition—phallus, vulva and womb—apply with unexpected perfection to Stonehenge.

Both these stone carvings would have been understood without difficulty by the symbol-makers of the Age of Stonehenge. In both, as in the mural from Neolithic Dorchester (see p.59), we are in the magical world of Divine Marriage by means of the symbolism of sexual union. In America it is the picture symbolism of a recent Neolithic age; at Dorchester the picture symbolism dates broadly from the same time period as the earliest phase of Stonehenge, when ditch and bank were constructed and the Heel Stone was assigned its nuptial position.

Whatever the situation may have been at that time in the fourth millennium, there was a later tendency throughout Europe for the dominion of early agrarian Great Goddesses to be reduced by the rising power of Sky Gods. They began as simple consorts, but increasingly tended to become potential, usurping warrior gods. The Beaker-using peoples may have assisted in spreading such changes, and indeed, the replanning of Stonehenge from 2000 BC onwards was the work of British Beaker forces and their descendants. If so, the thematic problem at Stonehenge may have been overcome by deifying the ancient Heel Stone as a Sun Stone, so that its powers might be wholly attributable to the work of the sun god. This deification would justify the cutting of the sacred ring about the stone instead of, or as well as, my previous suggestion that the ring kept the multitude from crowding too near the stone on midsummer's morning. Still later, even more sweeping changes were ruthlessly delivered, for the Late Bronze Age must have seen the complete annihilation of the priests and believers at Stonehenge by unnameable conquerors. Nothing less could account for the abandonment of such a well-beloved, precious monument and the ending of the age-old Divine Marriage ceremonies.

Be that as it may, the sarsen phase of Stonehenge rose in the Early Bronze Age at the hands of a race whose leaders appreciated luxury items of gold and bronze. They were the builders of the thousands of round barrows which cover the plains to this day; they were the men and women who inherited beliefs and a tradition which at least in the beginning embraced the divine phenomenon of the tornadic-whirlwind spirit. In the temperament of the age their homes were round dwellings, shaped like their tombs and henges, every one a microcosm of the circular universe, every one a sacred retreat with its own centre.

Their public spiritual centre was the circular temple of Stonehenge whose cyclopean construction was taken to completion because of the force and logic of a compelling religious theme. Its over-ambitious design and centuries-long construction could only have been realised by the exercise of an authoritative priestcraft which held the confidence of a powerful ruling class. Stonehenge was not the achievement of a world of shamans whose individualistic talents and use of magical powers belonged to the nomadic groups of northern Europe. The settling of communities and the spread of religious sites permitted priest-led organisations to develop, and Stonehenge was conspicuously the nucleus of the finest of these. The circles were constructed to manifest a people's sacred mythological beliefs by employing a principle which focused on a belief in Divine Marriage. The solemn rituals were re-enacted yearly, probably on the first day of a summer festival, in a vivid and comprehensible form, and with a brilliance, beauty and emotion which modern peoples cannot appreciate.

Nor was this the only British temple at which the Marriage of the Gods was so grandly celebrated. Not far north of Stonehenge is another colossus, the megalithic temples at Avebury.

13

The Goddess at Avebury

Avebury is the giant of the world's stone circles.

Stonehenge has the advantage in subtlety of planning and brilliance of execution, but Avebury cannot be matched for its immensity. At the height of its glory a ring of 98 megaliths lined the interior of a henge ditch which was cut over nine metres deep into the chalk rock and had a bank of similar volume outside it. There were four entrance causeways, and, inside, two additional megalithic circle complexes. The southern circle system was centred about a tall stone which William Stukeley called the obelisk. Like so many of Avebury's important stones, it is no more, destroyed in one of the fanatical anti-heritage outbursts with which prehistoric Avebury has had to contend.

At the centre of the northern circle were three megaliths in a special arrangement known as a cove. This word was introduced by Stukeley to denote a setting of three standing stones, close to one another but not touching, which he described as 'set upon the ark of a circle, regarding each other with an obtuse angle'. Since the time of John Aubrey and William Stukeley, who were the first antiquarians to describe the megalithic coves of ancient Britain, their purpose within the sphere of prehistoric religious ritual has remained a mystery, save for Stukeley's speculation that they were 'perhaps . . . intended . . . for a nich-like hemispherical figure, in some sort to represent the heavens . . . The altar properly lay upon the ground before this superb nich'. As there is no excavation

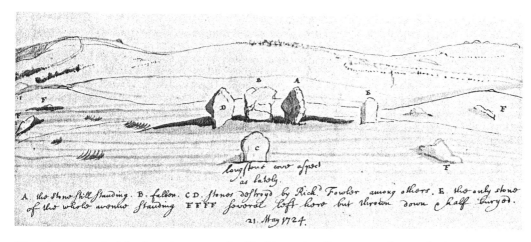

The stones west of Avebury known as the Beckhampton Cove according to the reconstruction by William Stukeley in 1724. Stone A of the cove and stone E of the avenue, which survive to this day, go under the names Adam and Eve. At the time of Stukeley's drawing stone B lay on its back, and a number of other megaliths labelled F lay fallen too. Stones C and D had recently been destroyed.

evidence for a missing altar stone, no megalith at Avebury has suffered the misnomer that has blighted terminology at Stonehenge.

The remains of two coves at Avebury survive to this day. Besides the one in the northern circle system, another, known as Beckhampton Cove, is to be found well to the west of the Avebury henge and circles, at a point along the great megalithic avenue called Beckhampton Avenue. By making use of the testimony and drawings of John Aubrey and William Stukeley there is no difficulty in compiling details of the positions and shapes of the cove's missing sarsens.

William Stukeley visited Avebury several times in the years to 1724. His drawing of the cove depicts the three stones D, B and A, and their positions on the northern side of the Beckhampton stone avenue relative to a fourth stone C located on the opposite side of the avenue. Stukeley remarked that one of the avenue stones (stone B) makes the back of the cove but it had toppled backwards. He also learnt that stones D and C had been 'carried off by that destroyer Richard Fowler' seven years earlier. Today only stone A survives, together with stone E, the last avenue stone remaining upright. Fortunately, this is enough to show that stone A stood at an obtuse angle of 110° to the missing back stone, which corresponds well enough with the situation as known for the North Circle Cove. Moreover, as far as one can tell, the back stone formerly faced the local midwinter sunrise, which is close to 130°.

The cove is plainly another sacred construction.

Stone A, the only surviving megalith of the Beckhampton Cove. It was one of a pair which stood either side of the Goddess Stone (stone B). Viewed from the direction of midwinter sunrise the shape of this broad massive stone becomes narrow and phallic.

The three cove-stones, and stone C facing them, appear to have obvious sexual qualities associated with the essentials either of masculinity (stones D, A and C) or of femininity (stone B). The surviving stone A, seen from the direction which emphasises its intended sexuality, is plainly phallic.

The inclusion of the male cove-stone C, which can be seen in William Stukeley's sketch, is crucial if we are to discover the reasoning behind the cove's construction, because by facing the female cove-stone B, stones C and B worked together as a Divine Marriage pair. Significantly, they were set on a common axis which seems to have been aligned on midwinter sunrise.

The local direction for the solsticial sunrise would be 128.4° for a distant level horizon, but because there is a nearby hill only three hundred metres to the south-east of Beckhampton Cove, which has an elevation of 1.4°, the time of local sunrise is delayed until the sun's azimuth swings to 130.5°. Curiously enough, and this could be the result of a deliberate decision, this direction also corresponds to the direction of an 18-metre diameter round barrow, Avebury 19b, built upon this hill. The barrow has not been excavated, so it is not known whether it is of Late Neolithic or Bronze Age date. If it is the latter, it would be much younger than the cove, but this need not preclude the possibility of a special siting, arranged late in the history of use of the cove, in order that it might serve as a solsticial marker. In this event one might expect the barrow to conceal an important burial in view of the high prestige occasioned by the midwinter alignment. William Stukeley included it in one of his drawings; today trees obscure it from view of the cove.

Because sunrise is delayed by some ten minutes, when the sun does come into sight the power of its rays has increased so much that, as it comes over the hill which is the near horizon, it immediately shines brightly on the pointed stone C, throwing its shadow directly on to the central cove stone (B). This carefully-planned orientation has immense implications for the purpose of stone C, because its status is raised enormously beyond that of a simple avenue stone. Stone C has to be reckoned as a functional part of the cove.

One may question the motives for siting a solsticial grouping of four colossal stones in the lee of a hill when any of so many other, seemingly better sites, with open prospects of the eastern horizon, could have been chosen instead. There must have been some pre-existing constraint, of which the most likely is that the planning of the cove was restricted in some way—in particular that it was dependent upon the design of the Avenue, the course of which had been decided or 'predetermined' by some other spiritual reasoning or divine force. The archaeological evidence that Beckhampton Cove and Avenue comprise the oldest part of the entire megalithic complex of Avebury lends weight to this theory. The date suggested for the Beaker burial by the cove, found by Maud and Benjamin Cunnington in 1911—broadly 2450–2300 BC—only dates the burial, not the cove or the avenue, which could be hundreds of years older. In fact, in Chapter 7 I proposed that the megalithic avenue might have been designed as a cursus substitute, which would mean that it was built long before the megalithic circles. Seeing that a vast number of megaliths were everywhere to hand, this proposal would explain why avenue-making was undertaken in an otherwise undesirable area in which watercourses only added to the already considerable engineering problems. After all, the cursus idea had swept the length and breadth of Britain so it would otherwise appear that the Windmill Hill people had been passed by. The way in which the Beckhampton avenue swerves to avoid the hill on its south-eastern, right-hand side is a known feature of some tornado paths. In the event that the position of the cove was restricted by the prearranged line of the avenue, the builders would have had to select from along the route of the curving avenue the most favourable position with which to align the solstice, irrespective of whatever quirks of topography might arise. If the cove had postdated the building of Silbury Hill, itself dated to the twenty-seventh century BC,

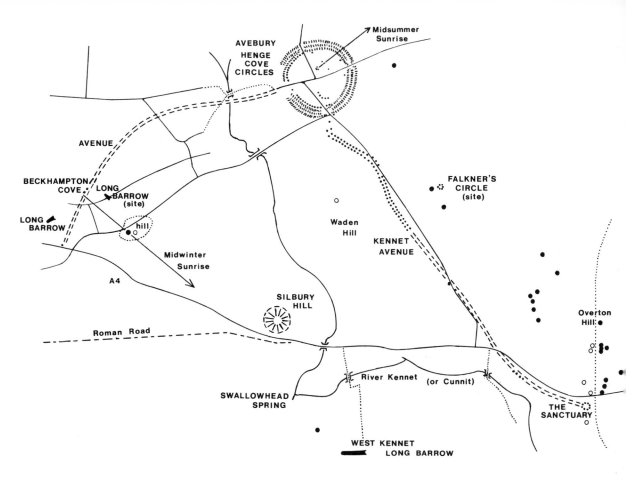

Neolithic and Bronze Age remains in the vicinity of Avebury. Note particularly the relationship between Beckhampton Cove and the midwinter sunrise over the hill to the south-east. If the cove was set on a pre-existing megalithic avenue, the cove's position can be explained by the criterion that the hill would delay the sunrise sufficiently to ensure that it was a bright sun which would come over the hillcrest. © *Crown copyright*

it could easily have been aligned on Silbury. Instead, Silbury Hill, although only 1.4 kilometres away, is out of sight on an orientation of 125° east of north.

In order to have an alignment geared to the winter solstice, a site for the cove would have had to be selected on the north-western boundary of the Beckhampton Avenue. Moreover, in order to have the cove's axis more or less at right angles to the line of the avenue, the choice of location would have been confined to that section of the avenue which extends a kilometre north-eastwards from where it crosses Nash Road which is the westerly extension of South Street out of Avebury Trusloe. The spot chosen was under Beckhampton Road hill in the direction of its rounded top, because this achieved the maximum elevation for the latter compatible with the fixed distance of the avenue from the hill. If it was not for the constraint of being limited to a pre-existing avenue, the cove could have been located nearer to the hill. The idea for this scenario may have been born from the functions and rituals which took place in its heyday at an earthen barrow adjoining South Street. Like all long barrows, the South Street barrow would have been raised to the glory of the Goddess, and we know from site plans that it, too, could have been aligned on the local midwinter sunrise, possibly for similar functional reasons centring around Divine Marriage ideas and festivals. In planning the cove, therefore, I believe the intention was to build an equivalent, in everlasting sarsen, of the old South Street long barrow which had been there for hundreds of years.

All priority was given, it seems, to seeking some presumably beneficial effect from having the cove on the avenue. If the latter was indeed the stone-lined equivalent of the ditch-and-bank cursuses of other communities, then the concept of Divine Union or hierogamy with the Sky God was already instilled into the sacredness of the stone avenue.

The principle of the winter-solstice alignment and its observance at the Cove of Beckhampton may be similar to that at the Thickthorn terminal of the Dorset Cursus, where the latter is skewed towards a midwinter-sunrise indicator in the form of the Thickthorn long barrow 200 metres distant. Concealed in the ditch-infill of the Thickthorn barrow, it will be recalled, were phalluses and other fertility symbols (and in the plough soil only a metre from stone A of Beckhampton Cove I found a lightly-worked ball-shaped flint, 60–70 millimetres in diameter, with circular and ovoid cross-sections). Furthermore, in the side of the Dorset Cursus towards Pentridge a long barrow was raised to face midsummer sunrise. By 3000 BC the tradition of building long barrows was waning, and with it the cult of ancestors; but the cursus culture was still in vogue and by the time of the earliest stages of megalithic 'Avebury' it was the cove that consorted with the avenue-cursus instead of a long barrow with a chalk cursus. It is even possible that the cove idea was discovered by accident. Because the megaliths were ordered in pairs, it may have been noticed that, at the position where the cove was later to be inserted, the angles of the turning avenue were such that it was at that one particular spot as the sun came over the hill on midwinter's day that the shadow of stone C fell upon its opposite number, stone B. To turn this arrangement into a cove would then only have needed the addition of the attendant male stones (A and D) at the sides of the female stone B.

The cove's objective was therefore to welcome and direct the New Year's sun into the avenue-cursus of a Goddess community, a society familiar with the expression of the concept of the Marriage of the Gods through the cursus-god beliefs. On midwinter's day the rising sun united male and female megaliths with the fertilising power of the shade projected by the intromission of stone C.

So at Avebury Divine Marriage is the theme, just as it is at Stonehenge.

The one-time union of the gods, commemorated by the construction of the avenue-cursus, was exalted in a new kind of structure that repeated the mystical event year after year. The cove re-enacted the Cosmic Marriage on midwinter's morning—New Year's Day in those olden times—a ceremonial occasion doubtless accompanied by a winter festival. The same element of astrobiology is present in the religion of both societies, high proof of the importance in their mythologies of sexual union between the Goddess and her God.

The symbolism is the regeneration of life. At the centre of the cove is the Goddess Stone (B) flanked by male consorts (stones A and D). At Beckhampton the Goddess appears as bestower and regainer of life. The triumphant beginning of the New Year brings satisfaction and renewed hope to the uncertain world of the primitive British farmer.

The second cove, inside the northern circle of the Avebury henge, has two stones remaining. This cove was built to stand at the centre of a megalithic circle, but most of its stones are missing. As William Stukeley remarked of the cove: 'It opens pretty exactly north-east, as at Stonehenge', which means, of course, in the direction of midsummer sunrise.

The survivors of the North Circle cove are arguably Avebury's finest stones. Their sexual characters are obvious. The central stone has the typical qualities of female-type megaliths. Viewed from the direction of midsummer sunrise, it displays a polygonal earthbound solidity and massiveness four metres high, which totally contrasts with the slender phallic shape of its taller companion. As for the missing third stone which fell in 1713, William Stukeley was informed by the locals that 'it was full seven yards long, of the same shape as its opposite, tall and narrow'. Thus, viewed from the front, the direction of midsummer sunrise, the middle stone is solidly feminine, its companions wholly masculine. It is indisputable that the shapes of these magnificent stones conveyed an impression of divine sexuality to the informed adorants of the age.

Again we are in the province of the Great Goddess and Earth Goddess. The cove comprised a massive Goddess Stone whose strength was augmented by the masculinity of her two consorts. She awaited the midsummer sunrise in the same fashion that her counterpart at Beckhampton awaited the winter solstice. Was she, too, served by the seed of an eclipsing stone's shadow? If so, this would provide the ultimate realisation of her manifold creative powers.

The answer is positive because it can be shown that a stone was once suitably positioned 22 metres to the north-east. Both Aubrey and Stukeley saw such a stone, a menhir labelled 'F' on Stukeley's plan, at some distance in front of the cove. On Isobel Smith's plan in *Windmill Hill and Avebury* the stone's orientation relative to the cove centre measures about 50° 00', which is the direction of midsummer sunrise when the sun climbs over Hackpen Hill four kilometres

A drawing of the Avebury Cove made by William Stukeley in 1723, looking south-west from a position next to a fourth cove stone known as Stone F. Stukeley has sketched in the position of the recently-removed third stone.

distant. William Stukeley showed the stone relative to the cove-stones in three of his sketches, as did Mr J. Browne of Avebury in a watercolour which he painted in 1825, three years before the stone's destruction by gunpowder.

The contribution of the fourth stone completes the scene of Divine Marriage at the cove. The stone's position, at 22 metres in front of the Goddess Stone, was placed just right so that it would eclipse the sun and provide a consummating shadow for the Goddess. To judge by the sketches and the painting, stone F appears to have been both broad and pointed, although it may possibly have been slightly broken by decay. Its breadth was approximately three metres and its height two-and-a-half to three metres above ground level. A three-metre wide stone at this place would subtend an angle of 7.5° as seen from the cove, but because the ground is lower there than at the cove, the section of its pointed end which used to rise above the skyline would have extended no more than two degrees horizontally and the same vertically.

What is more, the summit of stone F does not appear to have been centred precisely opposite the middle stone of the cove, but just a little towards the east,

The section of the great plan of Avebury drawn by William Stukeley, in which the relative positions of the cove stones including Stone F are shown.

much as the Heel Stone at Stonehenge is positioned slightly to the east of the midsummer-sunrise direction in order to ensure that the eclipse trick works. Consequently, as at the Beckhampton Cove where the cosmic intercourse takes place in midwinter, there is here, in the heart of Avebury, ample proof of a four-stone cove, in which the fourth stone provides the consummating shadow for celestial intercourse with the Temple Goddess on midsummer's morning.

On 15 June 1986 I witnessed a perfect midsummer sunrise at the cove. This date is only six days before the sun arrives at its most northerly position along the eastern horizon, the true midsummer morning of 21 June. The sun climbed over Hackpen Hill at 0407 GMT (0507 British Summer Time) which is about nine minutes later than it does at Stonehenge on account of the height of the hill. The eclipsing stone, had it been there, would not at first have interfered with the sunrise as viewed from the cove. As at Stonehenge, the sun rose unimpeded to the left of the estimated position of the 'sun stone', and illuminated the Goddess Stone with its rays. But very soon this phallic stone would have eclipsed the sun as the latter passed behind it, and for some minutes the Temple

Goddess would have enjoyed the shadow's embrace. About 0412 I took an unusual shadow photograph. Standing five metres in front of the Goddess, my shadow had a greenish hue, coloured by the lichen on the otherwise sun-reddened Goddess Stone.

The basic religious symbolism at Avebury's North Circle Cove is clear. The cove was the repository of the power of the Divine—and by consequence that of the priestesses and priests. What happened at the Goddess Stone was received as a manifestation of the divine before the worshipping populace. The vision of the Divine Marriage procured and intensified the belief of the people. On account of its position at the heart of the temple, this splendid stone—a transmutation of the Goddess who on this day appeared in her guise as the Womb Stone and was impregnated in parallel with similar events at Stonehenge no more than thirty kilometres to the south—must have been the most important stone at Avebury. Indeed it is almost the biggest-known stone idol to the Goddess raised in antiquity in Britain, and much more massive than the Womb Stone of the Goddess at Stonehenge. And, as with the Stonehenge Womb Stone, at times of high ceremonial the imagery becomes absolute, because the stone, then fully occupied by the soul and spirit of the Goddess, *is* the Goddess. As inheritors of the prehistoric landscape handed down to us by our ancestors, we are fortunate that this stone, more than any other at Avebury, has endured the attacks of narrow-minded discrimination and violence. This central megalith is as indispensable for a proper understanding of Avebury as is the Goddess's Womb Stone at Stonehenge, because both are Goddess Stones and the stones of Avebury's North Circle may be likened to a womb circle as is the horseshoe-shaped womb at Stonehenge.

At times of prayer or festival, in addition to the summer solstice, the Goddess might repossess and occupy the stone. Whatever the doctrine or method, whatever the mythological reasoning, the North Circle Cove was her shrine and residence. She was there to offer, as does a church, relief and refuge to sincere believers. At the summer solstice she was sought after and supplicated for her powers of controlling the fertility of the crops, to enrich the harvest and secure the health of animals and people. At Beckhampton Cove it was the winter solstice that was celebrated, as an insurance for the renewal of the world and the fertility of women and animals as the New Year arrived. The coves were holy places, the foremost shrines of the Windmill Hill people. Although not anthropomorphic, each Goddess Stone was nonetheless a Giantess of a divinity, recalling the Welsh Giantess 'Barclodiad Y Gawres' (meaning the Giantess's Apronful of Stones), the Neolithic temple on the coast of Anglesey. Her solid mass implanted in Earth, she is seen as a formless deity, and is the more powerful for being without the distractions provided by the imperfect outline of a human figure. She may look impersonal to us, but, unsculpted, her reality as the image of a Neolithic Goddess was touchingly personal.

The heart of Avebury is like the womb of Stonehenge: both monuments preserve omnipotent icons. The presumption would be that, as in India today, supplication attracts the celestial and earthly deities with the purpose of impregnating the cult images with their holiness. The idea of divine sexual union with phallus and vulva, or *lingam* and *yoni*, united stands for the driving force which runs the world. The Goddess cult reached India in Neolithic times as an eastward extension from the Near East and Europe.

From what we can tell, Neolithic India bore similarities with Neolithic Britain and Ireland, to which the farming immigrants coming from the Continent carried the cult of the agrarian goddess and the theory of the Marriage of the Gods, except that the cursus of the gods was a regional development peculiar to Britain, which at Beckhampton-Avebury was rendered in stone. Avebury's great rings were built at the eastern extremity of the earliest stone avenue, on what could have been holy ground sanctified by whirling spirits in the south-eastern lee of Windmill Hill, very like the vapour vortices and the glowing ionised vortices witnessed recently in the locality. The other megalithic circles known in the Avebury region (Falkner's circle, Langdean Bottom, Broadstones) could equally well have been consecrated following the appearance of the remarkable crop-circle phenomenon which at times is endemic thereabouts.

14

The Marriage Cult

The building of the great temples at Avebury and Stonehenge stemmed from the material and spiritual needs and immortal aspirations of anxious, pious peoples who were moved to stage-set their mythical imagery in a sensational scenario. Raised in dependable, timeless stone, the temples were intended to last for ever. Now that the hostility suffered by the Avebury megaliths in recent centuries has ended, and despite the lesser but unremitting attacks of the weather, the immutability and might of the remaining megaliths and the care of an enlightened society should guarantee their safety.

We can now see how the principle of the midwinter and midsummer Weddings of the Goddess at Avebury, made visually splendrous at the two coves, was anteceded by the mating principles inherent in the long-barrow traditions of the region.

The earliest long barrows, as at Horslip (on the side of Windmill Hill) and South Street (near Beckhampton Cove), were largely or wholly earthen mounds. South Street long barrow, which is under the low hill close by to the south-east, was orientated at least approximately and probably intentionally on the midwinter sunrise. The rather later barrows of East Kennet and West Kennet had megalithic chambers, the former, like Stoney Littleton thirty kilometres to the west, awaiting midwinter sunrise, the latter the equinoctial sunrises.

The barrows intended for the winter hierogamy awaited the most southerly rising of the sun along the eastern horizon. On our Gregorian calendar this turns out to be on or close to 21 or 22 December which is the shortest day. Throughout all Neolithic and Bronze Age prehistory the midwinter celebrations would have been around 21–30 December which by consequence of being the turning point for the sun, would have been thought of as New Year's Day. It was because this well-loved event in the European calendar could not be eradicated or displaced when the Christian missionaries arrived that they chose to celebrate Christ's birthday at this time as a convenient means of smothering its true origins.

The closure of the chambered long barrows in the Avebury region about the middle of the third millennium corresponded roughly with the debut of the Avebury stone circles and the rise of the coves. The still earlier earthen barrows may have served similar purposes as well, so a continuity of belief is discernible from the start of the fourth millennium to the end of the second millennium. A similarity of function would further emphasise that the ancient long barrows were not primarily built as tombs. They were Goddess shrines and their foremost purpose was as places of ritual and worship, with at certain times of the year celebration of the perennial theme of the Marriage of the Gods. In a region such as the Cotswold Hills, where there were dozens of fine chambered long barrows but no stone circles, we can see that it was the barrows which were the centre of attention on the great festival days, particularly the days when the Divine Marriage was welcomed and honoured.

To what extent was this rite built into Britain's other megalithic monuments? I am in the process of widening my research to cover all of Britain, Ireland and Northern France. The extent of the cult was countrywide, and was revealed in different ways at various times and places during the three thousand years for which visible evidence is available in the form of surviving monuments. I think it likely that the rite was universally understood and adored—in Neolithic Europe too—and was practised by all communities everywhere, even when no megalithic or other signs remain today.

There is at Stanton Drew, less than ten kilometres from the centre of Bristol in the west of England, a magnificent megalithic complex comprising three stone circles, a cove and other menhirs, which ranks third in England behind Avebury and Stonehenge. The theme of hierogamy seems to be suggested in the north-east circle. These stones consist of enormous blocks of silica-bearing brecchia (a rock of coarse composition), one of which, although now fallen, seemingly had the right azimuth for the sun at its midsummer rising to cast its broad shadow to the centre of the ring, where some sacred object or holy person might have been waiting. The arrangement could be deliberate, for the ground slopes strongly in the Stonehenge fashion but more markedly, which has the effect of shortening and strengthening the shadow. The circle once consisted of eight standing stones,

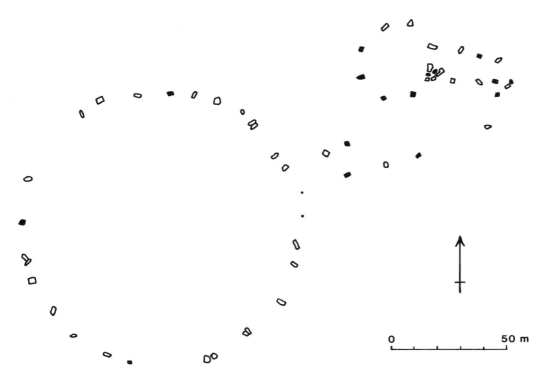

Circles and avenues at Stanton Drew south of Bristol towards the Mendip Hills. A third circle and the cove are off the map to the south-west. The stones are shown double size. The great circle has a diameter of 113 metres. *After L. V. Grinsell*

but as five are now fallen we cannot be certain of its exact shape. The diameter is nevertheless 30–31 metres, close to the diameter of the first Stonehenge and the Durrington walls timber circle, besides being one of the favoured diameters for large-diameter natural crop circles. The shape may be slightly elliptical, which is another common and understandable feature of vortex-formed crop circles. Site selection by the discovery of a spiral-centred crop-circle formation could have happened, in which case the Sacred Wedding principle would naturally follow, as noted many times in this book for other Goddess-religion examples.

From this circle a short avenue leads eastwards, more exactly on a bearing of 96 degrees from north. It is possible that this was formerly recognised as the alignment of the local equinox, but equinoctial bearings were not always evaluated well in prehistoric times because the sun was not at a turning point of its cycle. The great circle at Stanton Drew has an avenue too, with a middle bearing of 55° east of north, which approximates rather poorly with the local midsummer solstice, the hills to the north-east delaying the sunrise by a few degrees. A Sacred Marriage stone arrangement might have been intended within this structure, because when the sun is just above the horizon in this direction the long shadows of the avenue stones interlink with one another and join up. Similar ideas can be advanced for some other stone avenues, as at Callanish in the Outer Hebrides for the equinoxes (approximately). Added to the fine stone circle at Callanish at an obviously later date is an east-facing chambered cairn which is actually built within the small stone ring, also with a central pointed megalith. We must also allow for the fact that in some regions, before the advent of the megalithic period or where suitable stone was anyway lacking, sacred avenues were constructed using timber posts, but the positions of very few of these have been recovered.

Surprisingly but significantly, the local name for the Stanton Drew circles is the Weddings, a name which could hark back to the Neolithic and Bronze Age Sacred Marriage. In 1723 William Stukeley recorded, 'The noble monument is vulgarly called the Weddings and they say 'tis a company that assisted at a nuptial solemnity thus petrified'. A folk story tells how the stone rings were once the guests at a wedding feast, who became petrified for dancing on the sabbath. This story sounds very like a Christianised rendering of a still more archaic original dating from the time when the Sacred Wedding festival was a major annual event in the region.

The cove at Stanton Drew is placed on a straight line with the centres of the great circle and the north-east circle but not in sight of either due to an intervening ridge. Stukeley was told that traditionally the three stones of the cove were known as the parson, bride and bridegroom. Could this be a deformed folk memory surviving from prehistoric times—that one of the stones was indeed the 'bride', where Bride referred to the ancient Goddess and the main cove stone was her cult object? No evidence for a missing fourth stone has been recorded, nor does the cove face any sunrise position, but as Aubrey Burl points out, its direction approximates to the extreme southern moonrise. If it was a reunion with the moon that was intended, then a fourth stone (as at Avebury) might be dispensable, due to the weakness of the moon's shadow, and some other lunar device or rite invoked, as may have happened with the recumbent Goddess Stones at stone circles in Scotland.

At Arbor Low in Derbyshire a central cove faces the northern moonrise according to Aubrey Burl. Again, because of the feeble light of the moon, the shadow trick is ineffective and unnecessary. It sufficed that the Goddess Stones of these coves faced the desired moonrise, so that the Moon Goddess made contact nocturnally.

The cove at Stanton Drew today. The Goddess Stone lies in pieces, the male stones misshapen but still erect on either side.

In Oxfordshire, at the stone circle known as the Rollright Stones, Divine Marriage may also have been practised, but the position is unclear because some of the stones have been damaged or moved. Their number has even increased in the last couple of centuries. There is certainly an entrance to the circle from the 'midwinter' south-east direction, and a stone of the circle seems to stand in the 'midsummer' position at the north-east.

Another interesting site is Mayburgh, at Eamont Bridge, near Penrith in Cumbria. The high bank of this magnificent henge is made of pebbles and stones from the nearest river bed and valley. An entrance in the east admits the rays of the rising sun at the spring and autumn equinoxes. At the centre of the henge a magnificent megalith still stands, but missing are three near-neighbours which were to its north-east, east and south-east respectively as indicated on an old plan. It would be worthwhile to probe for the stone-holes in order to find their exact angles relative to what appears to be a very fine Goddess Stone. Not far away, on higher sloping ground near Little Salkeld, is the splendid megalithic circle known as Long Meg and her Daughters. Long Meg is a red sandstone

The stone circle and henge of Arbor Low, high in the Derbyshire hills, with the cove at its centre. Every stone of this once-splendid Goddess temple has fallen.

outlier placed in line with the midwinter sunset as seen from the centre of the stone circle. Its long shadow would stretch right across the centre of the circle as the sun went down for the night.

Cairnpapple, on a hill-site between Edinburgh and Glasgow, was another ritual centre which had a cove. The great circle at Stenness in Orkney has a damaged cove which faced the splendid Neolithic temple of Maeshowe. The nearby Ring of Brodgar may have boasted a cove, too, at what is now called the Comet Stone.

Many dozens of Goddess temples at which Divine or Sacred Marriage ceremonies took place can be identified across Britain, Ireland and France. Several based on megalithic architecture are listed in Table VI, chosen to give a representative selection from different parts of these countries. There are many more, besides non-megalithic barrows from all parts of Britain. These include the earthen barrows described in earlier chapters in connection with the Dorset Cursus and the Stonehenge Cursus. In some cases precise measurement of alignments is not possible—but precision of orientation may not always have been

The Goddess Stone in Mayburgh Henge with the eastern entrance beyond. Seven other megaliths which played their role in the scenario are missing.

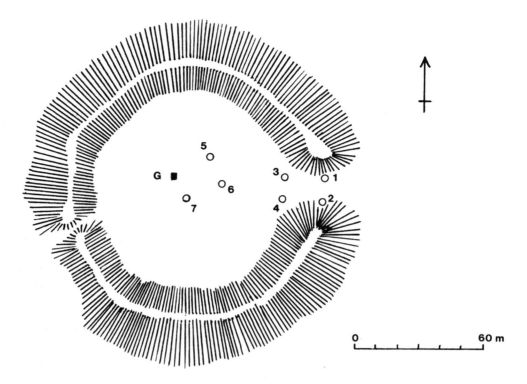

Map of Mayburgh Henge with stone positions according to Pennant. At the spring and autumnal equinoxes the sun shone through the vulvar gap between the entrance megaliths (stone 1–4) and consummated the Marriage with the Goddess Stone G by the phallic shadow of stone 6.

thought necessary by the prehistoric worshippers. If the date of the solstice could be determined by some other means, such as the use of horizon identification markers, then the monument served its primary purpose as religious precinct and temple. Furthermore, the ceremony of the Marriage of the Gods might have been celebrated by some communities on other days of the year as well, especially Imbolc (1 February), May Day, Lammas (1 August), and Samhain (31 October), so that some monumental or megalithic alignments may denote these solar directions instead.

Above all else, the barrows, like the circles, were Goddess monuments. In Cheshire near Congleton, there is an east-facing chambered barrow with crescent-shaped forecourt called the Bridestones, the name probably a relic of the Goddess herself via the ancient British Goddess Bride whose name lives on

TABLE VI
Some Goddess temples which seem to have been designed for Divine Marriage ceremonies

Name	County	Grid Reference	
Stonehenge	South Wilts	SU 123422	midsummer sunrise
Avebury, North Circle Cove	North Wilts	SU 103700	midsummer sunrise
Avebury, Beckhampton Cove	North Wilts	SU 089693	midwinter sunrise
East Kennet, barrow	North Wilts	SU 116669	midsummer sunrise
West Kennet, barrow	North Wilts	SU 105677	equinoctial sunrises
Stoney Littleton, barrow	Avon County	ST 735572	midwinter sunrise
Stanton Drew stone circles	Avon County	ST 601633	midsummer sunrise
Grey Mare and Colts, barrow	Dorset	SY 584871	midwinter sunrise
Hetty Pegler's Tump, barrow	Glos	SO 789000	midwinter sunrise
Nympsfield, barrow	Glos	SO 794013	midwinter sunrise
Randwick, barrow	Glos	ST 825069	midsummer sunrise
Hazelton South, barrow	Glos	SP 072188	midwinter sunrise
Heston Brake, barrow	Gwent	ST 505887	equinoctial sunrises
Addington, barrow	Kent	TQ 653592	midsummer sunrise
Kit's Coty, barrow/cromlech	Kent	TQ 745608	midwinter sunrise
Chestnuts, barrow	Kent	TQ 652592	equinoctial sunrises
Bridestones, barrow	Cheshire	SJ 906622	equinoctial sunrises
Bryn Celli Dhu, temple	Anglesey	SH 508702	midsummer sunrise
Swinside stone circle	Cumbria	SD 172883	midwinter sunrise
Mayburgh henge and stones	Cumbria	NY 519284	summer, winter, equinoctial sunrises
Temple Wood stone circle	Argyll	NR 827979	midsummer sunrise
Newgrange, temple	Co. Meath	Ireland	midwinter sunrise
Newgrange, temple	Co. Meath	Ireland	midsummer sunrise
Newgrange, temple	Co. Meath	Ireland	midsummer sunset
Knowth, temple	Co. Meath	Ireland	equinoctial sunrises
Knowth, temple	Co. Meath	Ireland	equinoctial sunsets
Dowth, temple	Co. Meath	Ireland	midwinter sunrise
Gavrinis, Larmor-Baden	Morbihan	France	midwinter sunrise
Ty-ar-Boudiquet	Finistère	France	midwinter sunrise
Les Mousseaux, Pornic	Loire-Atlantique	France	midwinter sunrise

Belas Knap, a chambered long barrow in the Cotswold Hills, Gloucestershire. Many Cotswold-Severn barrows have a true vulvar, trilithon entrance to the main passage, but at Belas Knap the vulvar idea persists although the obvious doorway is blind.

Dolmens and cromlechs, having a flat stone supported by vertical megaliths, present another aspect of Goddess imagery. While some may be the remains of earth-covered, galleried or single-celled long barrows, others were likely erected without any covering mound and may have changed little in the intervening years. This one is at Bodowyr, on the Isle of Anglesey, and has a typical womb-opening built to face the rising sun.

as the Christianised St Bride. The two-part terminal chamber of the Bridestones is divided by a 'port-hole' slab, which can be realistically interpreted as a womb-opening of the Goddess as at some of the Cotswold-Severn Goddess long barrows and French chambered barrows. The Cotswold Hills have fine examples of chambered tomb-temples facing critical directions between north-east and south-east, many or most of which could have served their communities as places for performing Sacred Marriage rites on various dates of the year. These even include long barrows with so-called blind entrances, as at Belas Knap (although in this case the celestial alignments are with side cells rather than the axis). This restored barrow in Gloucestershire has a deeply-horned forecourt, inset with a trilithon façade and backstone which allows it to be interpreted as a cove-like arrangement of stones. The same may be said of many of Britain's cromlechs which have a horizontal megalith supported head-high by three or more huge standing stones, such as Kit's Coty (Kent), Lanyon Quoit (Cornwall), Pentre Ifan (Dyfed) and Bodowyr (Anglesey) among dozens of others. Some may be the remains of megalithic long barrows, as is commonly supposed, but some were perhaps raised, just as we see them today, as Goddess-worshipping temples with no surrounding mound of earth. Their symbolic representation of the Goddess's womb-opening reminds us once more of the latter's simple beginnings thousands of years earlier in the Palaeolithic era, and its subsequent development and ultimate realisation at Stonehenge as the most elaborate of all images to the Great Goddess.

15

The Goddess... Then and Now

The solution to Stonehenge has been found, and with it a surprise, for it turns out that the monument, so long marvelled at for its mysteries and foreboding presence, has been storing a secret that concerns us all, one with a lesson for humankind.

We have seen how the peak of megalithic culture was reached by the building of ceremonial sanctuaries in which Heaven met Earth—centres which provided contact with the supreme divinities through manifestations materialising in timeless stone. The centrepiece of the ritual activity was the cult of the Great Goddess. In megalithic Britain and Ireland, as well as in Northern France, the Lady had always been known as a guardian divinity of the dead; now we have proof, revealed by the monuments themselves, that throughout the Neolithic Age her fecund powers were ascendant in the fields, in the animals, in women. At Stonehenge and at Avebury a remarkable ritual choreography was devised which united the heavenly powers of the Sun with the terrestrial dominion of the Goddess. The Cosmic Marriage had for a long time been a spiritual force. In a variety of forms it was celebrated everywhere that long barrows, henges, cursuses, circles and coves were built. By these sacred constructions monumental ceremonial reached the peak of its glory—and their supportive cultures lasted a further thousand years through much of the Bronze Age, before the warriors who built the Iron Age forts arrived with their importunate gods. Evidence of a celebration of Divine Marriage centred on a cult of the Goddess quickly diminishes after this, and wholly with the rise of Christianity, but in India and the Orient the archetypal Sacred Marriage continued and remains active to this day. The union of Indian Siva and Parvati, for example, was indeed another such wedding.

Throughout the prehistory of mankind primitive farming communities in all continents benefited from the reassurance and solace provided by mythologies inspired by the Marriage of the Gods. Recently recorded cases include tribal traditions from the North American continent where native Indians set down their beliefs in pictorial form—like the mating petroglyphs from California and Tennessee described in Chapter 12. As these dramatic concepts are merely the consequence of fundamental instincts deep in the psyche, their implications are open to psychoanalytical study, from which one finds that the Divine Marriage is an archetypal form at all levels of experience, one which ends in a fruitful, harmonious union. The marriage of Sun and Earth, or of Sun and Moon, is the unconscious symbolic joining of male and female principles which emanate from the psyche's congenital collective core. This is what makes the archetype so compelling and pervasive, why it so gloriously enriched the sacred symbolism of the Neolithic, why its sexual imagery appeals to free-thinkers so strongly today.

The truth and beauty of these revelations about the Goddess religions is all too obvious to open-minded people, but in the western world the anti-sexual stance established so long ago within Judaeo-Christian traditions inhibits true understanding. By coupling attitudes of sin and shame to what is, after all, just normal sexuality, no understanding of the divine attributes formerly expressed by genital-organ idols is possible for these believers. They have no feeling for the divinity once thought to be localised in these organs, no appreciation that the latter represented for the old religions, as Barbara Walker so vividly put it, 'a part of the gods' paradise miraculously embedded in human flesh'. This contrasts with the situation of the Tantra-reading Hindu who is at ease with nature and the cosmic obligation of uniting the principles which *lingam* and *yoni* define. By symbolising the male and female organs in conjunction the Tantric altar stone depicts the essence of the origin of life, and unashamedly declares that Goddess and God perpetually conceive to maintain the universe as we know it.

The Egyptian *sma* or *sam* amulet radiated the same message, the *lingam* or phallus in the *yoni* or vulva, while the mace—staff of office and symbol of authority known to the British Neolithic people with its beautifully carved and perforated bone or stone maceheads penetrated by a wooden shaft—originally bore the same significance, because its bearer owed his or her authority to the divine symbolism endowed in it by the principle of the Marriage of the Gods. This is not dissimilar from the orb and sceptre of today's regal authority, by

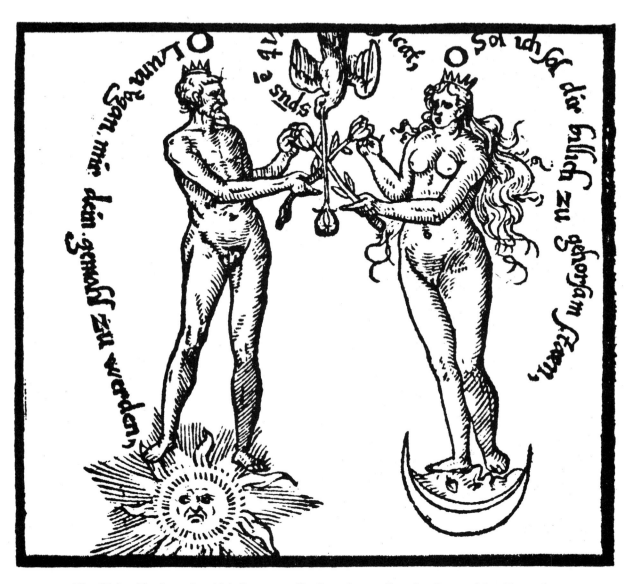

The Divine Marriage, in which the personification of opposites, the Sun and the Moon, the Sky Father and the Earth Goddess, achieve sublime communion in an archetypal blend of the Male and Female principles. A seventeenth-century Germany engraving.

which the spherical orb (standing for earth domination) held in the 'feminine' left hand, and the phallic sceptre held in the 'masculine' right hand, together symbolise the 'holy marriage' of monarch and country. In earlier times this Sacred Union was actually achieved by the wedding of the king with a priestess who personified the Goddess. As for the Yang and the Yin of the Chinese, Carl Jung declared that the intrinsic correspondence between the male and female principles—the complementary pairs of opposites called Yang and Yin—was substantiated philosophically by the ancient Chinese five thousand years ago; and he further noted that 'the oneness of man [sic] and the surrounding cosmos' displayed a deep regard of psychological fundamentals.

By celebrating the Marriage of the Gods the early societies were consciously blending archetypal images into a drama which typified their perennial fertility ambitions. Unconsciously, they were maintaining a coherent symbolic idea which arose in the psyche in primordial times, and is traceable back at least as far as 30000 BC, to the vulvar sculptures and art of the Upper Palaeolithic period with which I began this book.

I am hopeful that it will prove beneficial for humankind that Stonehenge, so long admired as an unfathomable ruin from a former age, and which stands serene and lonely in a God-fearing country, has been re-identified as the peace-loving, benevolent Goddess—Herself an everlasting image of harmony and love. Having survived the dark ages of three thousand years since its abandonment as a working model of the Goddess, Stonehenge may yet lead us back from a warring world and allow us to rediscover the social compatibility which should be achievable with balanced partnership societies.

In this monument we see a Holy Marriage of the Goddess whose consummation guarantees the fertility of the Earth. Its annual re-enaction reassures the community that the world is secure, and by demonstrating the unending cycle of life and continuance of the universe it maintains the everlasting immortality aspirations of the worshippers. The construction at Stonehenge is a working display and artistic statement of the life-generating union of sexual opposites which, by their conjunction, keeps the cosmic cycle in motion. Representing the whole Goddess in this drama, Stonehenge is an awe-inspiring tribute to Nature worship and love. For Goddess Worship is Nature Worship; and Goddess Love is Nature Love—the true and peaceful adoration of Earth and its mineral, vegetable and animal resources. Male-god worship imposes an unequal partition, arbitrarily enforced by male conquerors who have enjoyed thousands of years in a complacent and cruel suppression of half the world's population and who continually set at risk the entire world upon which we all depend.

The Goddess is alive because She is Nature, She is Earth, She is the World. This is our birthright, the consequence of millions of years of evolution. Whether we are religious believers or not—and no matter what we might think we believe —the Goddess *is* within us all through our love for and interdependence with Nature. Unconsciously or not, we have inherited and absorbed something of the ancient Goddess world, passed down to us through countless generations. For too long we have been deceived by a legacy of incomplete, often false historical information. Now that the Age of Right and Equal Rights is at last commencing, we must ensure that it achieves its aims, so long overdue, for the sake of our world.

Brilliant Stonehenge. Love, Power, Equality, Security, Fertility, Immortality —this is your message, the celebration of Life itself.

Bibliography

This select bibliography lists useful works on archaeology, Goddess religions and crop-circle science in which the reader can find additional details of the principal subjects treated in the text.

Stonehenge, Avebury and Their Times

ATKINSON, Richard J.C. (1979). *Stonehenge: Archaeology and interpretation.* Pelican, London (originally published by Hamish Hamilton, 1956).

BURL, Aubrey (1976). *The Stone Circles of the British Isles.* Yale University Press, New Haven and London.

BURL, Aubrey (1979). *Rings of Stone.* Frances Lincoln, London.

BURL, Aubrey (1979). *Prehistoric Avebury.* Yale University Press, New Haven and London.

BURL, Aubrey (1987). *The Stonehenge People.* Dent, London.

BURGESS, Colin (1980). *The Age of Stonehenge.* Dent, London.

CASTLEDEN, Rodney (1987). *The Stonehenge People.* Routledge & Kegan Paul, London.

CHIPPINDALE, Christopher (1983). *Stonehenge Complete.* Thames & Hudson, London.

CLARKE, D.V., COWIE, T.G., and FOXON, Andrew (1985). *Symbols of Power at the Time of Stonehenge.* HMSO, Edinburgh.

HEGGIE, Douglas C. (1981). *Megalithic Science.* Thames & Hudson, London.

MALONE, Caroline (1989). *Avebury.* Batsford, London.

RICHARDS, Julian. (1990). *The Stonehenge Environs Project.* Historic Buildings and Monuments Commission, London.

RICHARDS, Julian. (1991). *Stonehenge.* Batsford, London.

SMITH, Isobel F. (1965). *Windmill Hill and Avebury: Excavations by Alexander Keiller 1925–1939.* Oxford University Press, Oxford.

STUKELEY, William (1740). *Stonehenge.* London.

STUKELEY, William (1743). *Abury.* London.

UCKO, Peter J., HUNTER, Michael, CLARK, Alan J., and DAVID, Andrew (1991). *Avebury Reconsidered.* Unwin Hyman, London.

Goddess Religions and Comparative Religion

EISLER, Riane (1987). *The Chalice and the Blade*. Harper & Row, London.

ELIADE, Mircea (1958). *Patterns in Comparative Religion*. Sheed & Ward, London.

ELIADE, Mircea (1978). *A History of Religious Ideas: vol. 1. From the Stone Age to the Eleusinian Mysteries*. University of Chicago Press, Chicago.

GADON, Elinor W. (1989). *The Once and Future Goddess*. Harper & Row, San Francisco.

GIMBUTAS, Marija (1982). *The Goddesses and Gods of Old Europe: 6500–3500 BC Myths and Cult Images*. 2nd edn. Thames & Hudson, London.

GIMBUTAS, Marija (1989). *The Language of the Goddess*. Harper & Row, San Francisco. Thames & Hudson, London.

LERNER, Gerda. (1986). *The Creation of Patriarchy*. Oxford University Press, Oxford.

MEADEN, G.T. (1991). *The Goddess of the Stones*. Souvenir Press, London.

NEUMANN, Erich (1963). *The Great Mother: An Analysis of the Archetype*. 2nd edn. Princeton University Press, New Jersey.

WALKER, Barbara G. (1983). *The Woman's Encyclopedia of Myths and Secrets*. Harper & Row, San Francisco.

WALKER, Barbara G. (1988). *The Woman's Dictionary of Symbols and Sacred Objects*. Harper & Row, San Francisco.

Crop Circle Science

MEADEN, G. T. (1990). *The Circles Effect and its Mysteries*. 2nd edn. Artetech, Bradford-on-Avon, Wilts.

MEADEN, G.T. (1991). *The Goddess of the Stones*. Souvenir Press, London.

MEADEN, G.T. (ed.) (1991). *Circles from the Sky*. Souvenir Press, London.

OTHER REFERENCES

The works cited are listed under the first chapter to which they are appropriate although some appertain to more than one chapter.

Chapter 1. The Wonder of Stonehenge

EMERSON, Ralph Waldo. *The Problem*.

STEVENS, Edward T. (1882). *Jottings on Stonehenge*, p. 72. Brown and Co, Salisbury, England.

Chapter 2. The Universal Womb

BARBER, Chris. (1987). *Mysterious Wales*, p. 7 (fissured menhir in Wales at Maen y Cleddau).

BORD, Janet and Colin (1987). *Ancient Mysteries of Britain*, p. 238. Paladin, London.

CYRIAX, T. (1921). Ancient burial places. *Antiq. J.*, vol. 28.

DAMES, Michael (1976). *The Silbury Treasure*, pp. 110–12. Thames & Hudson, London.

DE VRIES, Ad. (1974). *Dictionary of Symbols and Imagery*, pp. 182–3. North-Holland, London.

FARMER, J.S., and HEMLEY, H.E. (1966). *Dictionary of Slang*, vol. 1. p. xxxi.

GIMBUTAS, M. *The Language of the Goddess*, p. 223 (pillar crypts). Harper & Row, San Francisco. Thames & Hudson, London.

GRAHAM, H. *Eternal Eve*, quoted by I. Opie and M. Tatem in *The Dictionary of Superstitions*, p. 199, Oxford University Press.

MUNSCH, J. (1986) has recorded triangular pieces of flint from the Early Palaeolithic which have had breasts and vulvas sculpted on them by knapping (a photograph is reproduced by Marija Gimbutas in *The Language of the Goddess*, p. 237).

OPIE, Iona and TATEM, Moira (eds.) (1989). *A Dictionary of Superstitions*. p. 199, Oxford University Press, citing *Folklore*, vol. 86 with regard to Brahan Wood, near Dingwall, in Ross-shire, Scotland.

WALKER, Barbara G. (1988). *The Woman's Dictionary of Symbols and Sacred Objects*, pp. 313–14. Harper & Row, San Francisco.

Chapter 3. Womb, Tomb and Temple

DARVILL, T.C. (1982). *The Megalithic Tombs of the Cotswold/Severn Region*, p. 26. Vorda, Highworth, Wilts. (Summarises the radiocarbon dating evidence for the Cotswold-Severn chambered barrows.)

ELIADE, M. (1958). *Patterns in Comparative Religion*, p. 412. Sheed & Ward, London.

EOGAN, G. (1986). *Knowth*, p. 147. Thames & Hudson, London.

Chapter 4. The Marriage of the Gods

CAMPBELL, Joseph (1974). *The Mythic Image*, pp. 38–9. Princeton University Press, New Jersey.

CIRLOT, J.E. (1971). *A Dictionary of Symbols*, 2nd ed, p. 189. Routledge & Kegan Paul, London.

DAVIDSON, H.R. Ellis (1964). *Gods and Myths of Northern Europe*, pp. 113–14. Penguin, London.

ELIADE, Mircea. (1958). *Patterns in Comparative Religion*, pp. 411, 412.

GIMBUTAS, Marija (1982). *The Goddesses and Gods of Old Europe*, pp. 228–30. Because the ithyphallic god from Casciarole is masked, Dr Gimbutas suggests that a festival is implied, at which a wedding is enacted, the male god marrying the Great Goddess.

GIMBUTAS, Marija (1989). *The Language of the Goddess,* p. 321.

GREEN, Miranda. (1986). *The Gods of the Celts*, p. 73. Alan Sutton, Gloucester; Barnes and Noble, Totowa, New Jersey.

MARSCHAK, A. (1972). *Roots of Civilization*, pp. 320–21. McGraw Hill, New York.

MELLAART, James (1967). *Catal Hüyük: A Neolithic town in Anatolia*, plate 83 facing p. 149. McGraw Hill, New York.

SCHNITGER, F.M. (1989). *Forgotten Kingdoms in Sumatra*. Oxford University Press, Oxford.

WESTROPP, H.M. and WAKE, C.S. (1875). *Ancient Symbol Worship*, p. 26. 2nd ed., republished 1972. Curzon Press, London.

WOODWARD, P.J. (1988). Pictures of the Neolithic: Discoveries from the Flagstones House excavations, Dorchester, Dorset. *Antiquity*. vol. 62, pp. 266–74.

Chapter 5. The Sky God Mates with Earth

AESCHYLUS. Frag. 44, *Tragicorum Graecorum Fragmenta*, ed. Nauck, p. 44.

CHRISTIE, P. (1963). The Stonehenge Cursus. *Wilts Arch Mag*, vol. 58, pp. 370–83.

CIRLOT, J.E. (1971). *A Dictionary of Symbols*, p. 315.

CRAWFORD, O.G.S. (1957). *The Eye Goddess*. Phoenix, London. (Refers to *Sumer 1*, plates III, IV.)

ELIADE, M. (1958). *Patterns in Comparative Religion*, p. 76 ff.

FRAZER, J.G. (1922). *The Golden Bough, A Study in Myth and Religion*, Ch. 15, abridged version.

LOVEDAY, R. (1985). *Cursuses and Related Monuments of Great Britain*. Unpublished Ph.D. thesis, Leicester University.

MEADEN, G.T. (1985). *Tornadoes in Britain*, p. 91. Commissioned Report for H.M. Nuclear Installations Inspectorate, Bootle, Lancs. (Available from their library.)

NEWMAN, Paul (1987). *Gods and Graven Images*, Robert Hale, London.

Phil Trans. Roy. Soc. (1731–2). Vol. 41, pp. 229–30. Relates to the Cerne Abbas tornado of 1731.

Quart. Journal Royal Meteorol. Soc. (1901). Vol. 27, pp. 251–2. Reproduces part of the original octavo pamphlet of the year 1729 concerning the Bexhill to Newenden tornado.

RICHARDS, J. (1984) in R. Bradley and J. Gardiner, *Brit. Archaeol. Report* no. 133, pp. 177–87. See also photograph in *Beyond Stonehenge*. 6. Trust for Wessex Archaeology, Salisbury (1985).

SMITH, A.C. (1860). *Wilts. Arch. Mag.* vol. 6, pp. 365–89.

STONE, J.F.S. (1947). The Stonehenge Cursus and its Affinities. *Antiq. J.*, vol. 104, pp. 7–19.

VIRGIL. *The Aeneid*. Book 4, pp. 165–6.

Chapter 6. The Path of the Sky God

ASHBEE, P. (1984). *The Earthen Long Barrow*. 2nd ed., pp. xxxiii–iv.

ATKINSON, R. (1955). The Dorset Cursus. *Antiq. J.* 29, pp. 4–9.

BILLET, H. (1914). The South Wales Tornado. *Geophysical Memoirs*, vol. II, Meteorol. Office, HMSO, London.

BRADLEY, R. (1986). *The Dorset Cursus: The Archaeology of the Enigmatic*. pp. 8, 16. Wessex Lecture III. Council for British Archaeology, Group 12, Salisbury.

BRADLEY, R., CLEAL, R., GARDINER, J., LEGGE, A., RAYMOND, F., and THOMAS, J. (1984). Sample excavation on the Dorset Cursus 1984. *Proc. Dorset Nat. Hist. and Archaeol. Soc.*, vol. 106, pp. 128–32.

BURL, A. (1987). *The Stonehenge People*. p. 115.

CIRLOT, J.E. (1971). *A Dictionary of Symbols*, p. 373.

CURWEN, E.C. (1929). Excavations in The Trundle, Goodwood, 1928. *Sussex Arch. Collections*, vol. 70, p. 32 ff.

DREW, C.D. and PIGGOTT, S. (1936). The excavation of Long Barrow 163a on Thickthorn Down. *Proc. Prehistoric Soc.*, vol. 1, pp. 77–96.

ELIADE, M. (1958) *Patterns in Comparative Religion*, pp. 99, 259.

ELIADE, M. (1969) *Images and symbols*, p. 41. Sheed & Ward, New York.

HEMP, W.J. (1935). The horned chambered cairn known as Bryn yr hen Bobl, near Plas Newydd, Anglesey. *Archaeologia*, vol. 85, pp. 253–92.

HOARE, R.C. (1812). *Ancient Wiltshire*, vol. i, p. 65. Inside the long barrow Warminster I 'at the south end was a sarsen stone five feet high, terminating almost in a point, and placed in an upright position'. Somewhat similarly a large conical sarsen once stood at the south side of the entrance to the Wor Barrow enclosure.

PENNY, A. and WOOD, J.E. (1973). The Dorset Cursus complex: a Neolithic astronomical observatory? *Arch. J.*, vol. 130, pp. 44–76.

PITT-RIVERS, A. (1898). *Excavations in Cranborne Chase.*

STARTIN, D.W.A. (1982). Prehistoric Earthmoving, pp. 153–6, in H.J. Case and A.W.R. Whittle, *Settlement Patterns in the Oxford Region*. Research Report 44, Council for British Archaeology, Ashmolean Museum, Oxford.

WAINWRIGHT, G.J. (1979). *Mount Pleasant Excavations 1970–71*, pp. 167–68. Thames & Hudson, London.

WHEELER, R.E.M. (1943). *Maiden Castle, Dorset*. Soc. of Antiq. Reps. of Research Committee.

Wiltshire Arch. Mag., vol. 46, p. 320, 1933, and vol. 47 p. 76, 1935.

Chapter 7. The Gate of the Gods

ATKINSON, R.J.C. (1953). The Neolithic long mound at Maiden Castle. *Proc. Dorset Nat. Hist. Arch. Soc.*, vol. 74, pp. 36–8.

BAILEY, C.J. (1971). An unrecorded enclosure on Martin's Down, Long Bredy. *Proc. Dorset Nat. Hist. Arch. Soc.*, Vol. 93, p. 168.

BAILEY, C.J. (1984). Fieldwork in the Upper Valley of the South Winterbourne. *Proc. Nat.*

Hist. Arch. Soc., Vol. 106, pp. 134–7.

BRADLEY, R. (1983). The bank barrows and related monuments of Dorset in the light of recent fieldwork. *Proc. Dorset Nat. Hist. Soc.*, Vol. 105, pp. 15–20.

BURL, A., (1987). *The Stonehenge People*, p. 94.

CORNWALL, I.W. (1953). *Proc. Prehistoric Soc.*, Vol. 19 pt. 2, pp. 129–47.

Current Archaeology (1969). No.1, pp. 2–4.

DYMOND, D.P. (1966). Ritual monuments at Rudston, East Yorkshire, England. *Proc. Prehistoric Soc.*, 32, pp. 86–95.

GRINSELL, L.V. (1959). *Dorset Barrows*, Plate IIa facing p. 18. Longman, London.

O'CONNELL, M. (1986). The Heathrow/Stanwell Cursus. *Current Arch.* Vol. 9, no 99, pp. 122–5. Tornado tracks can be long and narrow like this narrow cursus (width 20 metres); a recent narrow-path tornado track was the Grantham to Newark one of 8 October 1977. Observer reports suggested a width of 15–20 metres (see *J. Meteorology*, vol. 3, pp. 35–9, 40–2, and 143, 1978).

THOMAS, N. (1955). The Thornborough Circles, near Ripon, North Riding. *Yorkshire Arch. J.* vol. 38, pp. 425–45.

Chapter 8. The Stonehenge Cursuses

ASHBEE, P. (1984). *The Earthen Long Barrow*. p. 158.

BURL, A. (1987). *The Stonehenge People*, pp. 18 (Fig. 3), 19–20, 30, 62, 162.

HAWLEY, W. (1926). Report on the excavations at Stonehenge during the season of 1926. *Antiq. J.*, vol. 6, p. 4 (cf Burl A., *The Stonehenge People*, p. 97).

HOARE, R.C. (1810). *Ancient Wiltshire*, Vol. i, pp. 117, 157, 158. 'We next observed a rude conical pile of large flints, inbedded in a kind of mortar made of the marly chalk dug near the spot. This rude pile was not more than four or five feet in the base, and about two feet high on the highest part, and was raised upon a floor, on which had been an intense fire, so as to make it red like brick.'

MEADEN. G.T., and BROWN, P. (1979). *J. Meteorology*, U.K. vol. 4, pp. 201–2.

RICHARDS, J. (1984) in *British Archaeol. Report* no. 133, pp. 177–87.

ROBERTSON–MACKAY, M.E. (1980). A head and hooves burial beneath a round barrow on

Hemp Knoll, near Avebury, Wiltshire. *Proc. Prehistoric Soc.*, vol. 40, pp. 123–176.

STONE, J.F.S. (1947). The Stonehenge Cursus and its affinities. *Arch J.*, vol. 104, pp. 7–19.

THURNAM, J. (1869). On ancient British barrows. Part 1. Long barrows. *Archaeologia*, vol. 42, pp. 161–244, 182.

Chapter 9. The Henge of Stonehenge is Born

BURL, A. (1987). *The Stonehenge People*, pp. 62, 64–5.

Chapter 10. The Marvel of the Stonehenge Alignment

ATKINSON, R.J.C. (1978). Some new measurements on Stonehenge. *Nature*, vol. 275, pp. 50–2.

AUBREY, John. (1980–2). *Monumenta Britannica*, vol. 1, p. 93. Sherborne, Dorset.

BURL, A. (1987). *The Stonehenge People*, pp. 57, 78–9.

ELIADE, M. *The Quest: History and Meaning of Religion*, p. 33. Chicago and London.

PETRIE, W.M.F. (1880). *Stonehenge: Plans. Descriptions and Theories*. London.

SMITH, George (1973). Excavation of the Stonehenge Avenue at West Amesbury, Wiltshire. *Wilts. Arch. Mag.*, vol. 68, pp. 42–56.

WOOD, J.E. (1978). *Sun, Moon and Standing Stones*, p. 163. Oxford University Press.

Chapter 11. The Marriage is Consummated

GIMBUTAS, M. (1982). *The Goddesses and Gods of Old Europe*, pp. 227–30 (dates the Sacred Marriage concept in S.E. Europe back to 6500 BC at least).

Chapter 12. Goddesses of Stone

AUBREY, John (1982). *Monumenta Britannica*, vol. 1, p. 74.

BROME, James (1707). *Travels over England*.

BURL, A. (1985). *Megalithic Brittany*, p. 77.

BURL, A. (1987). *The Stonehenge People*, pp. 138, 186–7, 220.

CASTLEDEN, R. (1987). *The Stonehenge People*, p. 111; also R.J.C. Atkinson (1956) in *Stonehenge* (p. 77), on the need to remove the bluestones to some place of safety.

HAWKINS, G.S., and WHITE, J.B. (1966). *Stonehenge Decoded*, p. 82. Fontana/Collins.

HAWLEY, W. (1922). Second report on the excavations of Stonehenge. *Antiq. J.*, vol. 2, p. 50.

HAWLEY, W. (1924). Fourth report on the excavations at Stonehenge. *Antiq. J.*, vol. 4, pp. 30–9 (pp. 31, 37).

HAWLEY, W. (1925). Report on the excavations at Stonehenge during the season of 1923. *Antiq. J.*, vol. 5, pp. 20–50.

KEELER, Clyde (1978). Tree of life and labyrinth. *Occasional publications of the Epigraphic Society*, Arlington, Mass., vol. 5, part 2, article 107, pp. 27, 28.

PITTS, M.W. (1979). On the road to Stonehenge: Report on the investigations beside the A344—1968, 1979 and 1980. *Proc. Prehistoric Soc.*, vol. 48, pp. 75–132.

Chapter 13. The Goddess at Avebury

CAMPBELL, J. (1973). *The Masks of God. Primitive Mythology*. 2nd ed., pp. 24, 437. Souvenir Press, London.

GRAY, H. St.G. (1934). The Avebury excavations, 1908–22. *Archaeologia*, vol. 84, pp. 99–162. (Browne's painting faces p.101, there is a note on p. 108.)

SMITH, Isobel (1965). *Windmill Hill and Avebury*, p. 205, Fig. 70.

STUKELEY, W. (1743). *Abury*, pp. 23, 24.

Chapter 14. The Marriage Cult

GRINSELL, L.V. (1977). *Stanton Drew Stone Circles* (7pp. pamphlet). HMSO, London.

Index

Pictures in the text are indicated by italics. CP refers to colour plates.